Christine Schirrmacher
Thomas Schirrmacher

The Oppression of Women:
Violence – Exploitation – Poverty

WEA
World Evangelical Alliance

International Institute for Religious Freedom
IIRF

The WEA Global Issues Series

Editors:

Bishop Efraim Tendero, Philippines

Secretary General, World Evangelical Alliance

Thomas Schirrmacher

Director, International Institute for Religious Freedom,
Associate Secretary General for Theological Concerns, World Evangelical Alliance

Volumes:

"The WEA Global Issues Series is designed to provide thoughtful, practical, and biblical insights from an Evangelical Christian perspective into some of the greatest challenges we face in the world. I trust you will find this volume enriching and helpful in your life and Kingdom service."

Christine Schirrmacher
Thomas Schirrmacher

The Oppression of Women:
Violence – Exploitation – Poverty

An Existential Crisis for Millions

WIPF & STOCK · Eugene, Oregon

Wipf and Stock Publishers
199 W 8th Ave, Suite 3
Eugene, OR 97401

The Oppression of Women
Violence - Exploitation - Poverty
By Schirrmacher, Christine and Schirrmacher, Thomas
Copyright © 2020 Verlag für Kultur und Wissenschaft Culture and Science Publ.
All rights reserved.
Softcover ISBN-13: 978-1-7252-9438-7
Hardcover ISBN-13: 978-1-7252-9437-0
Publication date 12/4/2020
Previously published by Verlag für Kultur und Wissenschaft Culture and Science Publ., 2020

Contents

The Goal of This Book

The limited degree of gender equality enjoyed in Western countries exists for only a few other people on earth. Western countries have laws, educational opportunities, and sufficient affluence to pave the way for such a luxury. Generations past deserve thanks for this level of equality — those who campaigned for women and their rights. Such courageous women include our ancestor Käthe Schirrmacher and Bertha von Suttner, whose name marks a large square in the city center of Bonn, Germany, where we live.

From this position of privilege, a monument should be built for the millions of oppressed women around the world. It is neither a matter of promoting or restricting one or the other political or ideological camp, nor is it a matter of making a contribution to intra-feminist discussions, nor is it in any way a means to judge whether, in the short term, enough will have been done, since, as it stands, such thinking bypasses the brutal reality experienced in most countries on earth.

Nevertheless, all people of good will should take action jointly against human rights violations. Even worldview and ideological discussions about the contents of this book should not be allowed to thwart efforts taken against the evils mentioned, much less replace such efforts completely.

The third chapter goes briefly into the fact that there are not only women who suffer at the hands of violence. There are also violent women, and the appendix goes into how to evaluate the sometimes one-sided statistics. A reader should look at these sections first if this facet is important for assessing the numbers and facts used here.

This book seeks to present the discrimination and oppression of women around the world and to stir up a fact-based discussion. This brief space does not offer a lecture on solutions or on research regarding the various causes. Nevertheless, the hope remains that enough readers will be found who, driven by these distressing facts and injustices, will become active in politics, in human rights organizations, in development aid, or wherever they might have influence. As our ancestors have proven, change is possible when courageous people take action.

Violence Against Women

Why should we even occupy ourselves with violence against women? Isn't it clear that what we are dealing with is an issue involving injustice which nothing can justify? Though true in theory, practically speaking, violence against women is something which is omnipresent. It is not only found in distant Afghanistan but also right here in our midst. And it is found not only in private or in secret. It is found in many regions around the world as a part of everyday life, including the structure of society, the legal system, the separation of power, and resources. Furthermore, it has been propagated as justified or understandable in the minds of many people.

Violence against women is one of the most frequent human rights violations in all the world. But the problem is not only violence; there are nonviolent forms of oppressing women as well.

A scan of recent reports provides a grim snapshot. "The fate of a young Indian girl has unsettled the world for weeks. The 23-year-old student was raped by six men on December 16 [2012] in New Delhi, beaten with an iron rod, and then thrown out of a moving bus. She was hurt so badly that she died two weeks later. 'It regularly happens that a women is raped — and that she dies from her injuries,' stated Kristina Großmann, ethnologist and co-publisher of the recently released book entitled *Gewalt gegen Frauen in Südostasien und China* (English translation: *Violence against Women in Southeast Asia and China*). 'This current case is only the tip of the iceberg. That it is being publicly addressed is an exception.' In male-dominated India, sexual harassment is readily seen as a trivial offense, the rape of poorer women in rural areas is seen as routine, and these occurrences have, to date, hardly received public attention."[1]

Three men in Dubai in the United Arab Emirates recently sedated and raped an Australian woman. Then she was sentenced to eight years in prison for extramarital sex. In that country, the offenders would have had to confess, or four men would have had to testify as eye witnesses, in order for the offenders to be prosecuted.[2]

---

[1] Simone Utler, „Gewalt gegen Frauen: Diskriminieren, misshandeln, tabuisieren," *Spiegel Online*, 25 January 2013. http://www.spiegel.de/panorama/justiz/gewalt-gegen-frauen-vergleich-der-situation-in-verschiedenen-laendern-a-876618.html.

[2] Erica Ritz, "Horrifying: Australian Woman Gang Raped in Dubai – Then Jailed 8 Months for Sex Outside Marriage," *The Blaze*, 13 May 2013. https://www.theblaze.com/news/2013/05/13/horrifying-australian-woman-gang-raped-in-dubai-then-jailed-for-8-months-for-sex-outside-marriage.

In Japan, Toru Hashimoto, former mayor of the large city of Osaka, recently spoke about the many Asian women who were placed at the disposal of Japanese soldiers during World War II as forced prostitutes — euphemistically called "comfort women."

"In the circumstances in which bullets are flying like rain and wind, the soldiers are running around at the risk of losing their lives." He continued, "If you want them to have a rest in such a situation, a comfort-women system is necessary. Anyone can understand that."[3] Researchers estimate that the practice involved 200,000 — perhaps even 300,000 — women, mostly from Korea and China, but also from other occupied areas. For years, "comfort women" had to endure 30-40 men per day.[4] The victims have never been compensated.

Haven't the Western Countries Already Done Enough?

In 1911, only three countries allowed women to vote. Now, women vote almost everywhere elections are held, even in Iran. In 28 countries, 30 percent or more of the parliamentary members are women; in 19 countries, the elected head of state or head of government is female. The United Nations' Convention on the Elimination of all Forms of Discrimination against Women (CEDAW) has been ratified in 187 countries, even though occasionally with reservations. Paid pregnancy leave is guaranteed in 173 countries worldwide. Does this mean everything is all right?

Maternal mortality rates are compiled around the world according to set criteria.[5] According to these criteria, 37 mothers in Germany died during pregnancy or while giving birth in 2010. That amounts to five women per 100,000 live births — one of the lowest maternal mortality rates. Prior to World War I, the number ranged from 300 to 350; it peaked in 1929 with 550 mothers dying per 100,000 live births. In 2010, the global average was 210 women, with the average in industrialized countries between eight and 12 women. That figure was about 500 in Africa; in 2007, Nepal's average

---

3   "Japan WWII 'comfort women' were 'necessary' – Hashimoto," *BBC News*, 14 May 2013. http://www.bbc.com/news/world-asia-22519384.

4   Florian Stark, „Sexsklavinnen als Motivation für Japans Soldaten," *Die Welt*, 15 May 2013. https://www.welt.de/geschichte/zweiter-weltkrieg/article116209078/Sexsklavinnen-als-Motivation-fuer-Japans-Soldaten.html.

5   See the chart in Joni Seager, *The Penguin Atlas of Women in the World*, fourth edition (London: Penguin, 2008), 40-41.

was 870. Additional information about maternal mortality is in the second chapter.

This example demonstrates that, despite tremendous advances, the proper treatment of women can never be regarded as a personal or private matter. Such issues require involvement from society as a whole, including political efforts. A high maternal mortality rate seldom results from reprehensible actions by individuals; mortality rates stem from many different factors, many of which are beyond the influence of an individual. In a similar manner, the hard-won right of women to vote and serve in public office has been not only the result of individual actions; it has been part of a change in an entire society.

The World Economic Forum report on equality around the world ("The Global Gender Gap Report 2017"[6]) includes a ranking of 144 countries based on numbers relating to economic equality, access to education, access to health services, and participation in political life. For years, Iceland has held the first position. The first 20 spots are made up largely of northern and western European countries, as well as New Zealand, Rwanda, Philippines, Nicaragua, Namibia, Canada, Latvia, and South Africa. Switzerland holds the 21st position, Germany the 12th, and Austria the 57th. So, again: Does this show that everything is fine?

On one hand, much has been achieved. That is why this book does not focus on Western nations but on nations where women have seen no progress or even regression during the past two decades.

Obviously, marked progress does not mean nothing is left to be done in Western nations. Even today, far too many women are raped or otherwise sexually assaulted, forced into prostitution, or verbally insulted. And a glance at the 2017 report's rankings in the sectors of politics, business, health, and education shows how uneven our progress toward equality has been. Germany ranked 10th in politics, 43rd in business, 70th in health, and an embarrassing 98th in education. Switzerland's worst placement was 90th in education; Austria's was 84th in education. Of course, ranking criteria can be criticized, but they nonetheless indicate that very well-developed sectors can be accompanied by insufficiently developed sectors in the same country. For example, a country can have a long-term female federal chancellor and at the same time fail when it comes to fighting forced prostitution.

In the case of Germany, this can easily be shown in education. Generally, girls do better than boys in school, there are more female teachers

---

6   World Economic Forum, The Global Gender Gap Report 2017, http://www3.wefo
     rum.org/docs/WEF_GGGR_2017.pdf.

than male teachers, and there are more women than men studying in universities. There are almost exclusively female teachers in elementary schools, while in high school the numbers are about equal. However, the higher the level of education, the lower the percentage of women. Stated another way, it is not difficult for women in Germany to receive formal education, but it continues to be much more difficult for women than for men to become professors.

According to the German Federal Statistical Office, there were 10,500 female professors teaching at German universities in 2015.[7] This corresponds to 23 percent of faculty chairs, compared with 8 percent in 1995. Women made the strongest showing at 30 percent in linguistics and cultural studies, while the lowest was 9 percent in engineering. (Note that a bureaucratic 50 percent quota in professorial positions is not the answer; men and women may tend toward different interests for particular career groupings and topics and thus have different levels of involvement in different subjects. However, this does not explain the low number of female faculty chairs.)

Mean-Hearted Clichés

All major religions, worldviews, and cultures have at some point in their histories disdained or oppressed women, and there are many examples of how they have justified or substantiated such treatment. One Vietnamese expression states: "A man is ten times more valuable than a woman," while another states, "Regardless of how superficial a man is, he is still more profound than a woman."[8] An Islamic saying from the Near East says, "Men and women do not have the same value as people."[9] Arguably, there are similarly shocking statements found in all cultures, many coming from the mouths of the most eminent thinkers.

---

[7]   Statistisches Bundesamt (German Federal Statistics Office), „Frauenanteil in Professorenschaft 2015 auf 23% gestiegen," press release dated 14 July 2016. https://www.destatis.de/DE/PresseService/Presse/Pressemitteilungen/2016/07/P D16_245_213.html;jsessionid=7B63BEC97A7816A904DFF737C34D0B64.InternetLive2.

[8]   Genia Findeisen and Kristina Großmann, Gewalt gegen Frauen in Südostasien und China: Rechtslage, Umgang, Lösungsansätze (Berlin: regiospectra Verlag, 2013), 171.

[9]   P. Newton and M. Rafiqul Haqq, The Place of Women in Pure Islam (Caney: Pioneer Book Company, 1994[3]), 2.

Confucius (551-479 B.C.) upheld this, as did his student, writer and poet Fu Xuan (217-278 A.D.). Fu Xuan said: "How sad it is to be a woman!! Nothing on earth is held so cheap."[10] In Jewish morning prayer, men give thanks to God, "who did not create men as a woman."[11]

Misogyny on the part of many Christian church fathers, such as John Chrysostom (349-408 A.D.), has been widely documented. Almost 1,000 years later, religious teacher St. Thomas Aquinas (1225-1275) put another log on the fire: "The woman behaves to the man as imperfect and deficient (imperfectum, deficiens) to perfect (perfectum)," and "the main value of women lies in their ability to give birth and their benefit in the home." The high point of his misogyny consists in the following: "The woman is a blunder of nature . . . with her moisture surplus and her insufficient bodily temperature and intellectually inferior . . . a type of mangled, misguided, failed man . . . the complete realization of the human form is only the man."[12]

Renowned Koran exegete Ibn Kathir explains with respect to Sura 4:34: "Men are superior to women, and a man is better than a woman."[13] Likewise, ar-Razi, one of the most well-known Islamic theologians, passes judgment as follows: "Man is better than woman."[14]

The foundation of the hatred of women in German culture came from Plato; his student Aristotle produced the allegedly scientific justification for it. The history of philosophy is a history of the hatred of women; it re-bloomed during the so-called "Enlightenment" with figures such as Jean-Jacques Rousseau (1712–1778) and Immanuel Kant (1724–1804). Mary Wollstonecraft (1759–1797) was severely berated and maligned when, during the Enlightenment in France, she published *A Vindication of the Rights of Women* to augment the human rights that had just been adopted.

Atheism also brought forth bitter enemies of women.[15] Among the most severe formulations are surely those by Arthur Schopenhauer (1788–1860) and Friedrich Nietzsche (1844–1900). Nietzsche put the inclination for mistreatment of women in the classical words of oppression: "The happiness of man is, 'I will.' The happiness of woman is, 'He will.'" He called woman

---

[10]   This is the opening of his famous poem "Woman," found on various websites.

[11]   The various interpretive possibilities change nothing about the fact that one finds no corresponding thanks on the part of a woman for not being born a man.

[12]   All quotations from Thomas Aquinas, *Summa Theologiae*, Part 1, Question 92.

[13]   Ibn Kathir, quoted in Newton and Haqq, *The Place of Women*, 2.

[14]   Razi, quoted in Newton and Haqq, *The Place of Women*, 3.

[15]   See Hanna Barbara Gerl, „Frau und Mann in der Geistesgeschichte seit der Aufklärung," *Aus Politik und Zeitgeschichte* (Supplement to *Das Parlament*) No. B 14-15/91, 29 March 1991, 35-45.

a "slave" and a "tyrant," adding that "scholarly inclinations" among women were a sign of "disturbed sexuality."[16]

According to Karl Marx, "One should populate the world with boys,"[17] and "women apparently need custodianship."[18] His friend Friedrich Engels added: "However, I will not allow the little madams of women's rights to demand gallantry of us: If they want men's rights, they should allow themselves to be treated like men."[19] Engels also stated that Ferdinand Lassalle "has apparently gone to pieces due to the fact that he did not immediately take the person (referring to Helene von Dönnings) and throw her upon the bed and properly take her. She did not want his beautiful mind but rather his Jewish phylacteries."[20]

The United Nations and the Council of Europe

This is not the place to unfurl the story of women's rights or the legal situation in the German-speaking countries, but consider this short sketch regarding measures which have been taken by the United Nations and the Council of Europe against misogyny around the world. "On an international level, the topic has stood on the agenda for a long time. In 1979, the United Nations General Assembly adopted the Convention on the Elimination of All Forms of Discrimination against Women (CEDAW). In 1993, the General Assembly accepted the Declaration on the Elimination of Violence against Women. Since that time, sexual exploitation, genital mutilation, rape within marriage, abuse within the immediate social environment, dowry killings, selective abortions of female fetuses and forced sterilization, as well as state or state-tolerated physical, sexual, and psychological violence, all count as human rights violations. Up to the present time, 187 countries have ratified the CEDAW. However, in many cases it has been ratified with caveats – and in reality has not always been applied."[21]

---

[16]   Nietzsche quotations found in Gerl, „Mann und Frau," 39.
[17]   Karl Marx and Friedrich Engels, *Marx-Engels-Werke* (Berlin: Dietz Verlag, 44 volumes published between 1956 and 2018), vol. *34*, p. 388.
[18]   Karl Marx, *Marx-Engels-Werke 32*, p. 344.
[19]   Friedrich Engels, *Marx-Engels-Werke 37*, p. 137.
[20]   Friedrich Engels, *Marx-Engels-Werke 31*, p. 17.
[21]   Utler, „Gewalt gegen Frauen."

In 1994, the United Nations created the office of Special Rapporteur on Violence against Women, which has been affirmed multiple times and expanded.

The UN Resolution on Ending Female Genital Mutilation was resolved by the UN General Assembly on December 20, 2012. Therein, all 194 member states of the UN supported passing corresponding laws and strictly monitoring them.

Terre des Femmes, a Berlin-based nonprofit women's rights organization, wrote the following about the 2013 declaration: "On Friday, March 15, 2013, the 57th assembly of the UN Commission on the Status of Women ended in New York with a joint declaration on combating violence against women and girls. This obligated UN member states to equally protect the rights of women and girls as well as the rights of boys and men, thus to do away with discriminating regulations and practices of all types of violence. Furthermore, the murder of women on account of their gender is to forthwith be designated 'femicide.' Preventing and combating violence stood in the central focus of the year's UN Women's Rights Conference, which met from March 4-15. There were in total more than 2,000 female representatives from almost 200 governments, who came to an agreement for heightened awareness and measures for protection against violence towards girls and women, for the sexual self-determination of all people, as well as the right to gynecological care. The central point of contention in the negotiations was a formulation which said that neither tradition nor religious views justified violence against girls and women. It was, above all, Egypt, Iran, Libya, Sudan, Russia, and the Vatican which made a stand against these provisions up to shortly before adopting the declaration. In the last minute, however, they relented. There was also a compromise from the side of Western states, since the call for a right to homosexuality and sexual health was not incorporated into the paper in the end."[22]

The Council of Europe's Convention on Preventing and Combating Violence against Women and of Domestic Violence sets down that the equality of the genders must be anchored in the constitutions and legal systems of the signatory countries and that discriminating regulations have to be

---

[22]   Terre des Femmes, „UN-Frauenrechtskommission verabschiedet Erklärung gegen Gewalt an Frauen," https://www.frauenrechte.de/online/index.php/presse/ak tuelle-nachrichten/aktuelles-zu-frauenrechten-allgemein/archiv-fr-allgemein/1 154-un-frauenrechtskommission-verabschiedet-erklaerung-gegen-gewalt-an-fra uen.

abolished.[23] Additionally, offers of assistance to women, such as legal counseling, psychological care, financial advice, aid in achieving access to possible accommodation (establishment of women's shelters), training, and advanced training, as well as support in looking for work, have to be established. In addition, the signatory countries obligated themselves to work aggressively against forced marriages. In May 2011, 13 member states of the Council of Europe, including Germany, signed the Convention.

The Council of Europe's Convention on Ending Human Trafficking was developed in 2005, with the goal of strengthening the human rights of victims. It became operative in February 2008. Germany signed the Convention in November 2005 but only began to implement it in 2013.[24]

The Face of Violence Against and Oppression of Women

On the one hand, there is a history of hatred of women based on certain philosophical and religious views. On the other hand, there are good and noble words from the UN and Europe. Against this backdrop, let us turn our attention to the global reality.

In terms of absolute numbers, violence against women may well be the most frequent human rights violation. It is tremendously diverse, from abuse and rape in the most intimate realm of marriage to publicly visible gang rape in times of war; from the shameful and secretive abuse of children within a family to the violence against young girls that is glorified by German rappers and sold millions of times as entertainment.

In the final document of the Global Women's Conference in Beijing, the 1995 Beijing Declaration and Platform for Action,[25] the definition of violence against women, which largely follows the more significant UN Declaration on the Elimination of Violence against Women of December 20, 1993, is defined as follows:[26]

---

[23] Council of Europe, "Convention on Preventing and Combating Violence against Women and of Domestic Violence," 11 May 2013. https://rm.coe.int/168008482e.

[24] For more on international agreements regarding violence against women, go to the website of UN Women, Guiding Documents: http://www.unwomen.org/en/about-us/guiding-documents.

[25] United Nations, *The Beijing Declaration and the Platform for Action*, Fourth World Conference on Women, Beijing, China, 4-15 September 1995 (New York, 1996).

[26] United Nations General Assembly, 48/104, 85th plenary meeting, 20 December 1993, "Declaration on the Elimination of Violence against Women," http://www.un.org/documents/ga/res/48/a48r104.htm.

Definition: "Violence against Women"

"The term 'violence against women' means any act of gender-based violence that results in, or is likely to result in, physical, sexual or psychological harm or suffering to women, including threats of such acts, coercion, or arbitrary deprivation of liberty, whether occurring in public or private life. Accordingly, violence against women encompasses but is not limited to the following:

- Physical, sexual, and psychological violence occurring in the family, including battering, sexual abuse of female children in the household, dowry-related violence, marital rape, female genital mutilation and other traditional practices harmful to women, non-spousal violence, and violence related to exploitation;
- Physical, sexual, and psychological violence occurring within the general community, including rape, sexual abuse, sexual harassment and intimidation at work, in educational institutions and elsewhere, trafficking in women, and forced prostitution;
- Physical, sexual, and psychological violence perpetrated or condoned by the state, wherever it occurs."

Human Rights Violations against Women, according to Terre des Femmes

"Trafficking in women around the world as cheap labor, mail-order brides, and forced prostitutes, the failure to recognize women's persecution as a reason for asylum by virtue of gender, denying women the right to have self-determination over their bodies, e.g., forced sterilization and genital mutilation, sexualized violence towards girls and women, the abortion of female fetuses, dismembering and marketing the female body through genetic and reproductive technology."[27]

Violence against women is manifested on physical, sexual, psychological, economic, and social levels. Often it is relatives and acquaintances who commit acts of violence such as abuse, rape, or so-called harmful traditional practices (HTP), such as forced marriage, female genital mutilation (FGM), honor killings, or other offenses in the name of honor. The report on female poverty in the European Union states that "close to 20-25 percent of women of adult age are or have been exposed to physical violence, and more than 10 percent of all women are or have been the victims of

---

[27]   Terre des Femmes, „Frauenrechte weltweit," https://www.frauenrechte.de/on line/index.php/themen-und-aktionen/frauenrechte-weltweit.

sexual violence. .... Within the social environment, there are violent actions against women in the form of sexual harassment, sexual abuse, rape, the trafficking of women, forced prostitution, and forced labor. Force can also be exercised against women by the state and state institutions."[28]

It is estimated that on a global scale, six of ten women experience physical and/or sexual violence in some form over the course of their lives. A study by the World Health Organization (WHO) interviewed 24,000 women in 10 different countries and determined that in most countries, the percentage was between 30 percent and the global average of 60 percent. The percentages in the study ranged from urbanized Japan's 15 percent to rural Ethiopia's 71 percent.[29]

Unfortunately, comparable numbers regarding violence against men are harder to find. This one-sidedness often damages equality more than helping to improve the situation. This text will attempt to cite comparable numbers when available.

Numerous studies document that, viewed globally, violence against women is a major factor relating to death and disability, and in absolute numbers, it has worse consequences than, for instance, wars, cancer, malaria, or auto accidents. Unfortunately, the last comparative global study, widely reported in 2002 by the World Health Organization (WHO), is somewhat dated.[30] According to that comparison, more women ages 15-44 died worldwide from the consequences of violent acts — and also suffered more disabilities — than from cancer, malaria, auto accidents, and war taken together.

A 2011 study entitled "Violence against Women Prevalence Data: Surveys by Country," published by UN Women, presents data from 86 countries. These data are based on widely differing international, regional, and national studies. However, they demonstrates once again that violence against women is rampant around the world. According to a more recent study by WHO,[31] an average of 35 percent of women globally experience

[28]   Demokratiezentrum, „Gewalt gegen Frauen," http://www.demokratiezentrum.org/themen/genderperspektiven/lebensrealitaeten/gewalt-gegen-frauen.html.

[29]   "Strengthening Health System Responses to Gender-based Violence in Eastern Europe and Central Asia," http://www.health-genderviolence.org/training-programme-for-health-care-providers/facts-on-gbv/gbv-in-numbers/23.

[30]   This comparison originates from a World Bank report from 1994, "Violence against Women, Fact and Figures," http://www.enditnow.org/uploaded_assets/2563.

[31]   "Global and regional estimates of violence against women: prevalence and health effects of intimate partner violence and non-partner sexual violence" (Geneva:

violence or sexual violence, with 30 percent of all women experiencing this violence from their intimate partners. In the wealthy countries of Europe, the United States, and Australia taken together, on average 23.2 percent of women experience violence from their intimate partners. The corresponding averages from Africa, the Middle East, and Southeast Asia are around 36 to 38 percent.

With such prevalence, violence against women and girls has far-reaching consequences for the victims themselves, for their families, and for society as a whole. It damages the self-esteem, bodies, and souls of innumerable women, tarnishes their futures, and robs society of the possibility of having the next generation grow up in healthy family relationships with respect and esteem.

This violence also has a lofty price tag. A 2003 report by the U.S. Centers for Disease Control and Prevention calculated that the medical costs within the U.S. stemming from domestic violence amount to USD 4.1 billion. In addition, related workplace absences cause a USD 1.8 billion loss.[32] In 2015 the Australian government calculated that violence against women and children costs the country AUD 21.6 billion annually (about USD 17 billion).[33]

For a long time, in particular with respect to intimate relationships, violence was viewed as a private affair, in which the state and the public should not become involved. Often the legal means were lacking. This remains the case in many countries, where women run the danger of being charged with having extramarital relationships if they report rapes or of becoming victims of honor killings if they seek to charge their husbands. Additionally, police and other security forces used to be, and in many places still are, heavily male-dominated and ill-prepared to handle these cases.

However, the central task of the state must be to protect the dignity, life, integrity, and human rights of all citizens, regardless of who has to be

---

World Health Organization, 2013). http://www.who.int/reproductivehealth/publications/violence/9789241564625/en/; See also Benjamin Knaak, „Jede dritte Frau in Europa ist Opfer von Gewalt" (translation of title: Every third woman in Europe is the victim of violence.), *Spiegel Online* 4 March 2014. http://www.spiegel.de/panorama/gesellschaft/eu-studie-frauen-erleben-haeufig-psychische-und-physische-gewalt-a-956872.html.

[32] "Costs of Intimate Partner Violence Against Women in the United States," Centers for Disease Control and Prevention (Atlanta, GA, 2003), p. 2. https://www.cdc.gov/violenceprevention/pdf/IPVBook-a.pdf.

[33] https://www.vichealth.vic.gov.au/media-and-resources/media-releases/violence-against-women-costing-australia-over-20-billion-dollars-a-year.

protected or how close the culprit is to the victim. The less women are able to defend themselves, or the more dependent they are economically or otherwise, the more the state has to protect them, as well as all who are weak. This responsibility begins with clear laws and necessary enlighten-ment; such responsibility extends to effective criminal prosecution and in-tensifies with the energetic elimination of societal conditions that pro-mote violence.

Domestic Violence

The most dangerous place for women and girls is the very place where they should be safest — within their own families and homes. Admittedly, the term "family" often is broadly defined in domestic violence studies, and the use of "common household" would be a better term. As early as 1993, the U.S. Department of Justice determined in a more precise analysis that five percent of rapes against women were committed by their husbands; 21 percent by their civil partners, ex-husbands or ex-civil partners; 56 per-cent by relatives or friends; and 18 percent by individuals unknown to the victims. More recent studies indicate similar results, though unfortunately the breakdown of offending groups seems somewhat arbitrary. For exam-ple, one could ask why friends and relatives are not shown separately.

Regardless, this is not an isolated problem. Women around the world are affected – even if to strongly varying degrees. According to Amnesty International (AI), surveys conducted for *The Penguin Atlas of Women in the World*[34] between 2002 and 2007 show that, depending on the country, be-tween 11 percent and 80 percent of women said they had experienced vi-olence from their partners. The lowest percentage came from the Nether-lands and the highest from Pakistan. Russia and Bolivia follow with 70 percent each. According to this study, India has a rate of 42 percent, and Germany 20 percent, though a 2004 study on behalf of the German govern-ment, based on 10,000 interviews, found a level of 25 percent.[35]

[34] Joni Seager, *The Penguin Atlas of Women in the World.* Fourth edition (London: Pen-guin, 2008).
[35] Utler, „Gewalt gegen Frauen."

Percentage of women interviewed who said they experienced physical violence from their partners during 2002-2007[36]
[the six countries with the highest percentages:]

Pakistan	80%
Russia	70%
Bolivia	70%
United Arab Emirates	66%
Nigeria	66%
Turkey	58%
...	
USA	31%
...	
Germany	20%
...	
Lowest level: the Netherlands	11%

Results of the 2004 Bielefeld University study regarding Germany

1. Physical and sexual violence is predominantly domestic violence committed by a partner, ex-partner, family members, close friends, or neighbors.

2. The phase prior to and after separation is the most dangerous for women.

3. Violence occurs equally in all classes across various levels of education, and this applies to offenders and victims.

4. Women of Turkish descent, of whom 38 percent are affected, are more frequently affected than German women, of whom 25 percent are affected.

Gewalt gegen Frauen in Paarbeziehungen. 4th Edition. 2012:
https://www.bmfsfj.de/bmfsfj/service/publikationen/gewalt-gegen-frauen-in-paarbeziehungen/80614?view=DEFAULT.

---

[36]   According to Seager, *Atlas of Women*, pp. 28, 29.

Among the most troubling problems is that family attitudes in some cultures make women feel that violence against them is justified.

Percentage of women finding violence against them acceptable[37]	
Egypt	94%
Zambia	91%
India	70%
Ethiopia	69%

Here are some examples:

- "Men and women are equal on paper [in China] according to the sixth article of the Constitution adopted in 1950, and domestic violence is forbidden through the revised marital law dating from 2001. And yet, according to a study conducted in 2010 by the All China Women's Association (ACWF), 50-60 percent of all divorces in the People's Republic of China are motivated by domestic violence."[38]
- A 2013 survey of 3,500 men by Kirikale University in Turkey found that 28 percent of males consider violence against their wives to be normal. Thirty-four percent "occasionally" find it to be "necessary." And 30.9 percent want to beat their wives only when there is "good reason."[39]

But violence within a woman's own four walls is hardly just a problem in areas with limited female education or cultures that condone — or at least insufficiently punish — violence toward women.

Even when the overall figures improve, women — particularly those in households led by a single mother — bear the brunt of domestic violence. A 2012 study[40] by the U.S. Department of Justice found that between 1994 and 2010, the rate of partner violence sank by 64 percent to 3.6 occurrences per 1,000 partnerships for victims age 12 and older. This included men and

---

[37]   According to Seager, *Atlas of Women*, 28-29.
[38]   Utler, „Gewalt gegen Frauen."
[39]   "Domestic violence OK sometimes: 34 percent of Turkish men," *Hürriyet Daily News*, 16 April 2013. http://www.hurriyetdailynews.com/domestic-violence-ok-some times-34-percent-of-turkish-men-44974.
[40]   Shannan M. Catalano, "Intimate Partner Violence, 1993-2010," *Bureau of Justice Statistics*, 27 December 2012. https://www.bjs.gov/index.cfm?ty=pbdetail&iid=4536.

women, but four victims out of five were female. The highest rate of violence was among those ages 18-24 and 25-34. Women and girls in households with a single mother were ten times more likely to be victims than were individuals in households comprised of a married couple with children. Women and girls in a household with a single mother were six times more likely to become victims than were those in households comprised of a single female without children.

A 2002 report by the Austrian Federal Ministry of Social Security and Generations estimated that when including unreported cases, between one in five and one in ten women living in a relationship was affected by serious violence. Two-thirds of murders were committed in the immediate family, and the victims were women and children in 90 percent of murder cases.[41]

In Germany, 49.2 percent (154 out of 313 cases) of women killed were the victims of their current or prior partners, according to 2011 data from the Federal Criminal Police Office (Bundeskriminalamt, or BKA). "Women are in the most dangerous situation in their own home. This is the case all around the world, and it is also the case in Germany."[42] Domestic violence is the most frequent cause of injury when it comes to women: This occurs more frequently than automobile accidents and cancer combined. For women, the risk of experiencing violence at the hands of a partner in a relationship is far greater than that of being physically assaulted by a stranger. Education, income, age, and religious affiliation are completely irrelevant. Every fourth woman is or has been the victim of domestic violence. Her own home is the most dangerous place for a woman."[43] Violence by men against women and girls costs German society several billion euros annually, as there are costs arising for the justice system, the police, medical treatment, and for absence from work.[44] In 80-90 percent of all cases,

---

[41] „Häusliche Gewalt," (translation of title: "Household Violence") https://de.wiki pedia.org/wiki/H%C3%A4usliche_Gewalt (13 May 2013), after verifying the sources.

[42] On the situation in Germany and Switzerland, see the studies presented in Christine Ockrent, *Das Schwarzbuch zur Lage der Frauen: Eine Bestandsaufnahme* (translation of title: The Black Book on the Situation of Women: An Inventory; Zurich: Pendo, 2007), 334-341.

[43] Terre des Femmes, „Häusliche und sexualisierte Gewalt" (translation of title: "Domestic Sexualized Violence") https://frauenrechte.de/online/index.php/the men-und-aktionen/haeusliche-und-sexualisierte-gewalt.

[44] Brandenburgische Technische Universität, „Kosten Häuslicher Gewalt in Deutschland" (translation of title: "The Costs of Domestic Violence in Germany"), 28 November 2017. https://www.b-tu.de/news/artikel/13210-kosten-haeuslicher-ge walt-in-deutschland.

women are the victims of domestic violence and men the offenders. Every year, approximately 40,000 women and their children in Germany flee to women's shelters, and many have to be turned away because of insufficient space for them.[45]

The establishment of shelters for abused women was slow in coming. The first women's shelters emerged in the Anglo-Saxon world at the end of the nineteenth century, founded by Protestant social reformers and feminists. Most of these shelters disappeared over the course of the twentieth century, when it also seemingly became taboo to discuss violence in marriage. For example, between 1939 and 1969, the specialist publication *Journal of Marriage and Family* did not publish a single article on the topic. But 1970 brought a worldwide wave of outrage. In Germany, the first shelter for women opened in 1976; rape within marriage finally became a punishable offense in 1997. In 2002, the Protection against Violence Act (Gewaltschutzgesetz) was extended to include information about and penalization for sexual violence in the domestic sphere.

Rape

One of the worst forms of violence against women is rape. There is still the false belief that rape is triggered by unsatisfied sexual desire and is most natural in societies with restrictive public morality. Rape, however, is an expression of power and the dramatic demonstration of one's supposed strength at the cost of the woman to degrade her. Sometimes rape can be revenge on women in general as compensation for a perceived injustice which has been suffered. Generally, the sexual offender suffers from weak self-esteem, is not capable of a relationship on an equal footing, and acts as an expression of misogyny.

It cannot be emphasized enough that rape is not a sub form of sexuality but rather a form of violence. Rape does not have to do with satisfying one's sexual drive but rather with a drive for power, and it is for this reason that one aptly speaks of "sexualized violence."

Around the world, rape often occurs in those places where women should experience protection and help.[46] Too often it occurs in police stations, in the army, and in prisons, in broad daylight, or in areas which are

---

[45]   Petra Kaminsky, „Häusliche Gewalt: Was tun, wenn der Partner zuschlägt?" (translation of title: "Domestic Violence: What to do when your partner attacks?"), T-online 27 July 2017. http://www.t-online.de/leben/liebe/id_51015476/haeusli che-gewalt-was-tun-wenn-der-partner-zuschlaegt-.html.

[46]   See the chart in Seager, *Atlas of Women*, 58, 59.

removed from sight. Most frequently, however, rape occurs in the home environment of one's personal circle of friends or acquaintances.

According to an older and extensive representative survey by the United States Department of Justice for the period 1993 to 1995, 91 percent of the victims of rape were female and 99 percent of the offenders were male.[47] The Department of Justice examined all reports of rape by children and adolescents for the years 1991 to 1996. Ninety-four percent of the offenders were male, and 82 per cent of the victims were female, whereby as the age of the victim progresses, the relative proportion of female victims and the proportion of male offenders rises.[48]

The terrible crime of rape occurs very frequently, but getting reliable numbers about the exact frequency is notoriously difficult, because so many rapes go unreported. We can get at least a vague idea of how many women suffer in this way by mentioning a disagreement between two government departments in the United States. The U.S. Department of Justice estimates the number of rapes per year within the U.S. at approximately 300,000.[49] In contrast, the U.S. Centers for Disease Control estimate that the number of rapes per year within the U.S. is close to 1,300,000, meaning the CDC is counting one million more rapes per year within the U.S.[50] The world population is between 20 and 25 times that of the U.S. Without knowing which U.S. number is more reliable and without knowing which countries have rape percentages higher and lower than the U.S., one can estimate that globally there are many millions of rapes per year, probably tens of millions.

Of all countries, it is Sweden, where equality is far advanced, which has the highest rape rate in Europe. There were 46 rapes per year per 100,000 inhabitants in 2009, whereby one must note that the definition of rape appears to go beyond what is defined as rape in other countries. The behavior

---

[47] Lawrence A. Greenfeld, *Sex Offenses and Offenders: An Analysis of Data on Rape and Sexual Assault* (Washington, DC: Bureau of Justice Statistics, 1997). https://bjs.gov/content/pub/pdf/SOO.PDF.

[48] Howard N. Snyder, *Sexual Assault of Young Children as Reported to Law Enforcement: Victim, Incident, and Offender Characteristics* (Washington, DC: U. S. Department of Justice, 2000). https://www.bjs.gov/content/pub/pdf/saycrle.pdf.

[49] Patricia Tjaden and Nancy Thoennes, *Extent, Nature, and Consequences of Rape Victimization: Findings from the National Violence Against Women Survey* (Washington, DC: U.S. Department of Justice, 2006) iii. https://www.ncjrs.gov/pdffiles1/nij/210346.pdf.

[50] "Nearly 1 in 5 US women have been victims of sexual assault, CDC finds," *The Guardian* 14 Dec 2011. https://www.theguardian.com/world/2011/dec/14/1-in-5-women-report-sexual-assault.

of the media, the definition, and the practice of publication of information about rape vary greatly from country to country. Also, it is very seldom that the numbers relating to women are viewed in relation to the numbers for male victims. In Germany, the number of known rapes has dropped slightly and was at 8.9 cases per 100,000 inhabitants in 2009, approximately 7,300 reported rapes per year.

A representative study dating from 2004 and commissioned by the German Federal Ministry for Family Affairs[51] came to the conclusion that as an adult, every seventh woman in Germany was at one point raped, and more than half of those who had been raped (56 percent) were raped multiple times. For all practical purposes, the offenders were all male (99 percent). Eighty-five percent of the offenders came from the woman's personal environment, and only 15 percent of the offenders were unknown to the woman. Ex-partners were named most frequently. Resistance, calls for help, and fleeing were more frequently successful when the offender was unknown to the victim than when the offender came from the victim's personal environment.

South Africa has the highest rape rate in the world. The chance of learning to read is lower than that of being raped. Every year there are more than 64,000 cases of rape reported. Police and women's associations, however, estimate that the number of unreported cases is 10 to 25 times the official numbers. If a larger study correctly shows that only every twentieth rape is reported, that would mean that there are 1,300 women who are the victims of rape every day. That yields a total of 475,000 women per year. In South Africa, every fourth woman is the victim of sex-related violence. In a survey which was conducted, every fourth man admitted to having committed a rape in the past. Convictions are rare.[52]

A study in Ecuador reported that 37 percent of school girls who have experienced sex-related violence in school indicated that their teachers were the offenders. Hardly any such cases have been reported.

"In 1993, the United Nations Convention on the Elimination of all Forms of Discrimination against Women was ratified [by India], and in 2005

---

51   *Lebenssituation, Sicherheit und Gesundheit von Frauen in Deutschland* (German Federal Ministry for Family Affairs 2004), 79. https://www.bmfsfj.de/blob/84328/0c83aa b6e685eeddc01712109bcb02b0/langfassung-studie-frauen-teil-eins-data.pdf.

52   Claudia Bröll, "Aufschrei in Südafrika," *Frankfurter Allgemein,* 8 March 2013. http://www.faz.net/aktuell/gesellschaft/kriminalitaet/nach-vergewaltigungs tod-aufschrei-in-suedafrika-12056200.html. "Sexuelle Gewalt in Südafrika: Mädchen aus Kapstadt stirbt nach Vergewaltigung," *Süddeutsche Zeitung,* 10 February 2013.   http://www.sueddeutsche.de/panorama/sexuelle-gewalt-in-suedafrika-maedchen-aus-kapstadt-stirbt-nach-vergewaltigung-1.1595918.

strict laws against domestic violence were adopted. Thus, on paper, there is much that has been done in India. However, the will to introduce a change of awareness with respect to the position women have still seems to be missing. According to a study by the organization TrustLaw, the country is among the 20 leading developing and emerging countries in which the rights of the female population are the least protected: In almost 90 percent of the officially reported violent crimes, one woman or more were the victims. After the rape of a female student in New Delhi, however, things are happening. There has been a hotline for the victims of sexual crime since January 1 [2013], and the government has appointed two commissions which are to work out suggestions for improving the security of women. There is supposed to be new lighting in New Delhi, and buses are to be better monitored. In addition, the police are attempting to train more women for police service so that the victims of rape can more easily turn to the authorities."[53]

The Libyan dictator Muammar el-Qaddafi, who in the third chapter of his *Green Book* conjured up a form of equality, not only held for himself a brutal female set of body guards he designated disarmingly as the Amazonian Guard. Rather, like rulers 3,000 years ago in the Orient, or like 1,000 years ago among the Incas, he had masses of young women from all over the country brought before him, from among whom he then chose some whom he raped and kept captive in a cellar for weeks. Using eye witnesses, Annick Cojean wrote a book entitled *Gaddafi's Harem* as a monument to the victims.[54] It is no surprise that Qaddafi also punished his subordinates and intimidated them by raping their wives and daughters and that the regime employed rape as a terror measure against dissenters. It is also no surprise that the dictator himself sometimes raped men as punishment.

Gang Rape

A still worse act than rape is gang rape, whereby one or more women are raped serially by a group of men, one after the other. If we follow the International Handbook of Criminology, the following insights can be outlined:[55] 1. The act is mostly planned, thus not occurring spontaneously. 2. For the most part, the offenders are on average younger than in the case

---

53   Utler, „Gewalt gegen Frauen."
54   Annick Cojean, *Gaddafi's Harem* (Berlin: Aufbau, 2013).
55   Hans Joachim Schneider et al, *Internationales Handbuch der Kriminologie: Besondere Probleme der Kriminologie* (De Gruyter, 2009), articles on „Vergewaltigung" and „Gruppenvergewaltigung," 821-822.

of a single rape. This has to do with point 3: That gang rape mostly has to do with a collection of offenders with a strongly hierarchical structure, whereby the newer, weaker members have to demonstrate their strength. This pressure goes hand-in-hand with what criminologists call "collective irresponsibility." This leads to crimes being committed together which all individuals or most of the individuals in the group would not be capable of committing alone. However, within the group dynamic, perverse values of manhood, power, perseverance, self-assertion, and aggressiveness increasingly escalate. The group's norms, and the resulting shame if those norms are not fulfilled, become the key drivers of the crime.

Victims in the case of gang rape are not only humiliated because of the rape frequency. The humiliation has much more to do with the other group members' spurring on the act. Additionally, what is already a feeling of helplessness on the part of the victim is greatly heightened by the numerical superiority of the offenders. The physical and psychological damages are much more pronounced and last longer than in the case of an isolated act.

Gang rapes on the internet are often presented on innumerable pornographic sights and glorified without meeting any noteworthy protest. Depictions of group sex ("gang bang") often exhibit a large amount of violence. In the case of the gang rape mentioned at the outset, which occurred in the Indian city of Delhi on December 16, 2012, and drove tens of thousands of Indians out onto the streets in protest, the 23-year-old Jyoti Singh Pandey was raped and abused by six men. She died on December 29, 2012, from the effects of internal injuries. In India, rapes are often committed in groups and euphemistically called "Eve teasing."[56]

Rape During War

Violence against women on a massive scale has for millennia been an almost natural side effect of all wars and civil wars. It also occurs where states exhibit a weakly developed legal and judicial system and lawlessness is rampant. As if that were not alarming enough, one must note that this factor has tended to increase rather than decrease over the past 100 years. World War II surpassed World War I in this matter, but the Balkan conflict

---

[56] See „Gruppenvergewaltigung in Delhi 2012," at https://de.wikipedia.org/wiki/Gruppenvergewaltigung_in_Delhi_2012. See also "2012 Delhi gang rape:" https://en.wikipedia.org/wiki/2012_Delhi_gang_rape.

and the civil wars in Rwanda and Sierra Leone stand for systematic atrocities where women and girls were raped, forced into prostitution, held as child soldiers, or murdered. It is frightening to think that even UN troops, who are there to guarantee human rights and ensure peace, have in part been involved, as has been documented by official UN reports.[57]

It is well-known that rape is never more frequent than when committed by soldiers in time of war.[58] Rape in times of war is not only a sign of war's brutalizing and disinhibiting nature, especially since punishment is hardly feared. Rather, it is a means of demoralizing the enemy. Sex-related violence against women is systematically employed in almost every war or civil war as a means of conducting war. In 2008, the United Nations expressly determined this to be a fact and condemned it based on the report.

"Sex-related acts of violence against girls and women during armed conflicts have been known since antiquity, and up to the present day their use as a weapon of war has gone undiminished. In 1975 Susan Brownmiller demonstrated precisely in her standard work *Against Our Will* that rapes are an elementary component of every warlike conflict and, as a rule, do not require an order. However, it is a systematic weapon employed against respective enemies. Wherever men conquer territory, they also take possession of women's bodies. While rape in times of peace is meant to humiliate and destroy the women, rape in wartime has beyond that the function of destroying the 'us-feeling' on the part of the enemy's group."[59]

When civilians are affected by a war or civil war, it is women who overall suffer more than men. However, at this point it especially extends to systematic violence against women, and it is committed to achieve military, political, and/or psychological goals, to spread terror, to satisfy soldiers, to demonstrate hatred against ethnic groups, to produce offspring from their own ethnic group, or to prove that one is stronger and more powerful. In addition, there are rapes which occur because public order has broken down and there is no punishment to be feared. At that point the offenders are not only military opponents.

In addition, war crimes against women are often affected by their being played down and by their taboo nature. For certain, there were also other

---

[57] Ockrent, *Schwarzbuch*, 378-386 and the literature mentioned 601-602.
[58] See the list of cases 1991-2009 in Lydia Cacho, *Sklaverei: Im Inneren des Milliardengeschäfts Menschenhandel,* trans. Jürgen Neubauer (S. Fischer Verlag, 2011), 209-210. See also UNICEF, "Sexual Violence as a Weapon of War," https://www.unicef.org/sowc96pk/sexviol.htm.
[59] Frauen Helpline, „Kriegsvergewaltigung – sexuelle Gewalt als Waffe," (translation of title: War Rape: Sexual Violence as a Weapon), https://www.helpline-sh.de/kriegsvergewaltigung/.

areas and crimes in World War II which, for example, were hardly mentioned later to one's own children, but no area was hushed up like violence against women. Only over the past 20 years has there been any true research conducted on this issue and reports made regarding it in the media. It has to do with the innumerable rapes by German soldiers in conquered territories, which cannot even be estimated, as well as the estimated 1.9 million rapes by members of the Red Army in the conquered eastern areas and in Germany's eastern territory at the end of the World War II.

In addition, it often lasts a long time until the massive violence against women brought on by wars recedes, and then society remains more prone to violence than before. Supplying prostitutes and forced prostitutes on a large scale led to large bordellos during the Vietnam War and the Kosovo War which still exist decades later. The unknown port city of Pattaya in Thailand, where many soldiers in Vietnam spent their "leave" during the war, is to this day one of the largest bordellos in the world, as it was during the Vietnam War, which started Western sex tourism to Thailand in the first place.

In addition to uncontrolled rape which occurred during World War II, there were also forced bordellos, bordellos in concentration camps, German armed forces bordellos, Japanese war bordellos, and the systematic rape of inhabitants of the Chinese capital Nanjing by Japanese occupation forces in 1937.

It is repeatedly especially emphasized from the side of the military that rape is a "regrettable side effect" of war. In contrast, there are the statistics: The conservative estimates of historians in connection with World War II assume at least 2,000,000 rapes alone on German soil – of them, approximately 240,000 led to the immediate death of girls and women. The estimates of rapes by German soldiers on Russian soil has been estimated at about 10,000,000.[60]

In any case, one should add that for the most part in the statistics, there is no breakdown made between women and children, meaning that next to the larger percentage of girls, there are also underage boys included in the count. Overall, it is minors who make up the major victim group, and in Africa they make up at least 50 percent of the victims, according to Save the Children.

In the conflicts in the Balkans at the beginning of the 1990s, in Bosnia and Herzegovina as well as among the Kosovo Albanians, it is estimated that in each case 20,000 to 50,000 women were raped. The Second and

---

[60] See „Kriegsvergewaltigung" above.

Third Congo Wars (1998 – 2003, 2006 – 2009) are also bad examples.[61] In the civil war in Darfur in western Sudan, the "Janjaweed," an armed Arab-speaking, mounted militia, committed systematic rape on the black African population.[62]

Only since the middle of the 1990s has mass rape been internationally recognized as a war crime, and only since then has it been recognized that it is not only traceable back to unrestrained soldiers. For the first time in history, the ad-hoc International Criminal Tribunal for the former Yugoslavia (ICTY, located in Den Haag since 1993) and the International Criminal Tribunal for Rwanda (ICTR, located in Arusha, Tanzania, since 1994) brought charges for rape as war crimes and as crimes against humanity. In 1988, the Rwandan tribunal defined rape and sexual violence as genocide when they occur with the intention of destroying a particular population group.

As a result, three individuals were charged in 2001 with mass rape and sexual enslavement. In the judgment which was passed, their actions were classified as a serious breach of the Geneva Convention and categorized as a crime against humanity. In 2008, the United Nations Security Council adopted Resolution 1820, according to which sex-related violence in armed conflicts generally represents a criminal offense.

Rape During Civil War

What applies to formal war also applies to civil war within a country, and it likewise applies to revolutions and unrest of all kinds.[63] Mass rape during the American Revolutionary War has been well researched.[64] Along the way to democracy in connection with the fall of the Indonesian dictator Suharto, there was mass rape of Indonesians of Chinese descent.[65]

---

[61]   See the film directed by Susanne Babila, *Im Schatten des Bösen. Der Krieg gegen die Frauen im Kongo.* (translation of title: In the Shadow of Evil: The War against Women in Congo), television documentary by the German television channel SWR (Südwestfunk), in cooperation with Arte, 2007.

[62]   "Sudan, Darfur: Rape as a weapon of war: Sexual violence and its consequences," http://web.amnesty.org/library/Index/ENGAFR540762004.

[63]   Susan Brownmiller, *Gegen unseren Willen: Vergewaltigung und Männer Herrschaft* (translation of title: *Against Our Will: Rape and the Rule of Men*, Frankfurt: Fischer, 1994; original 1980), 115-137.

[64]   Brownmiller, *Willen*, 116-120.

[65]   Genia Findeisen and Kristina Großmann, *Gewalt gegen Frauen in Südostasien und China: Rechtslage, Umgang, Lösungsansätze*, (Berlin: Regiospectra Verlag, 2013), 47.

It is striking that extreme groups always grant themselves the right to rape the girls and women of the population groups they reject, even if racist separation is part of their ideology. The Nazis' SS raped Jewish women, and the Ku Klux Klan raped African-American women, although the prohibitions on sexual relationships with these population groups were respective parts of their agendas.

The UN special rapporteur for human rights reported that during the 1994 genocide in Rwanda, as many as 250,000 to 500,000 women and girls may have been raped, many of whom were raped many times.[66] In the Democratic Republic of the Congo, from 1996 onward, there have been 200,000 documented cases of rape, and the estimates of the actual number are much higher.

There were girls and women who were regularly raped – mostly in public – in attacks on villages by the Revolutionary United Front (RUF) and then made into forced recruits during the civil war in the African country of Sierra Leone from 1991 to 2002. "There was a preference for mistreating female family members of alleged enemies. Through the public (mass) rapes, the offenders attacked the masculine self-image of the respective male family members, who in their defenselessness were ridiculed as losers. RUF fighters also raped men in order to emasculate them. Likewise, the men who where raped they were occasionally mistreated by female RUF combatants. In this manner, sex-related violence was a widespread tactic of war used to break the long-term family and social cohesion of the respective enemies."[67] Estimates assume 215,000 to 270,000 female victims, of whom about 90,000 became infected with HIV.[68]

"More than five decades of civil war in Burma have led to violence becoming a part of the culture. Women are increasingly the victims. Indeed, after the elections in 2010 the military government promised a process of democratization, but there has been no change in awareness regarding women's rights and no reduction in violence. Although the government has ratified the United Nations Convention, it has not put it into practice

---

[66]   Report on the situation of human rights in Rwanda submitted by Mr. René Degni-Ségui, Special Rapporteur of the Commission on Human Rights, under paragraph 20 of resolution S-3/1 of 25 May 1994, paragraph 16. http://hrlibrary.umn.edu/commission/country52/68-rwa.htm.

[67]   Rita Schäfer, „Kriegerische Männlichkeit" (translation of title, "War-time Masculinity"), *Aus Politik und Zeitgeschichte* (APuZ 46/2009), Bundeszentrale für Politische Bildung (Federal Agency for Civic Education). http://www.bpb.de/apuz/31630/kriegerische-maennlichkeit?p=all.

[68]   See the sources cited in Schäfer, footnote 15.

in its national legislation. There are also no indications that laws against discrimination will be passed."[69]

"The report by Save the Children quotes, among others, a study in Liberia, according to which 83 percent of all victims of sexual violence during the civil war from 2011 to 2012 were under the age of 17. An additional study refers to the victims of sexual violence after the civil war in Sierra Leone. There, more than 70 percent of the crimes involved girls under the age of 18. According to statements by Save the Children, a large problem is that there is far too little money available for AIDS programs for the affected children and adolescents."[70]

Rape during civil war is not only directed at girls and women by the opposing side. It has been shown that brutality within the Palestinian Intifada also led to a strong increase in rape and honor killings of young Palestinian females by Palestinians.[71]

Rape in the Armed Forces

One could think that the topic of rape in war is limited to a demonstration of power by the victor toward the conquered or at least that rape within the army only occurs where there is no functioning constitutional state. Far from it! Rapes are no exception in the armies of democratic states. As long as it was the case that soldiers and officers were only men, rape, similar to the situation in male prisons, mostly affected weaker men. Female personnel accompanying armies have always been raped. However, since more and more women serve in armies, the rape of women soldiers and officers has become a growing problem.

What is particularly horrifying in this connection are studies conducted in the USA: It documents that incidents of rape in the military have been increasing since women have been allowed to become soldiers. Most of the victims do not report the incidents, however. Almost twenty percent of the women in the US Air Force Academy had been sexually assaulted, but 80 percent of the victims of rape had not reported the incidents when

---

[69] Utler, „Gewalt."
[70] „Vergewaltigungsopfer sind vor allem Kinder" (translation of title, "The Victims of Rape Are Primarily Children"), *Focus Online*, April 10, 2013. https://www.focus.de/politik/ausland/kriegsgraeuel-kinder-als-opfer-sexueller-gewalt_aid_957312.html.
[71] Stéphanie Le Bars in *Le Monde*, cited by Ockrent, *Schwarzbuch*, 72-77.

they occurred.[72] The estimated number of unreported rapes annually in the various branches of the United States armed forces is estimated to be 10,000 men and 9,000 women, whereby the percentage of women involved is much higher, since they still make up a smaller number. In 2012 there were 3,223 reported cases, 529 of the offenders were convicted by military courts, and 175 are serving terms in prison.[73] Up to now, one of the problems associated with reporting an assault had been that senior officers were able to suspend an investigation. It was only recently that this privilege was abolished.

"The US military has a relatively high percentage of women – 14.6% are female. However, a good track record with respect to career opportunities for females stands in contrast to an alarming report on incidents of sexual assault. . . . According to the United States Department of Defense, there were 3,374 cases ranging from sexual harassment up to rape in 2012 – an increase of 6 percent within two years. . . . An anonymous survey by the Pentagon revealed that the estimated number is significantly higher. According to the survey, 90 percent of sexual assaults are not reported. The reason for this is that the military has an absolutely poor record when it comes to prosecuting and convicting sexual offenders. Susan Burke, a lawyer who has defended a number of victims, has said that women who defend themselves have to reckon with career disadvantages and stigmatization. 'Revenge against the victims often ends by their [the victims, ed.] being pushed out of the military. The victims are ostracized, their performance assessments turn out worse, and what is said about them is that they are not capable of working on a team. Thus, it requires a good deal of courage to file a report. Less than 1 percent of the accused are convicted, but the probability of career disadvantages for the victim is very high. Since the United States military has not managed to master the problem over the course of two decades, the probability that the prosecution of sexual offenses will be detached from the military hierarchy is very high. There is in this case a political consensus in Washington, which is otherwise seldom non-partisan."[74] The reason for this is that there were two recently initiated proceedings against officers who had been deployed to, of all places, the department to combat sexual abuse. One of the individuals

---

[72]   Diana Jean Schemo, "Rate of Rape at Academy Is Put at 12% in Survey," *The New York Times*, August 29, 2003. https://www.nytimes.com/2003/08/29/us/rate-of-rape-at-academy-is-put-at-12-in-survey.html.

[73]   According to Schneider, „Vergewaltigung," 823, 834.

[74]   http://www.dradio.de/dkultur/sendungen/ortszeitaktuell/2107041/.

had supposedly forced a subordinate into prostitution, and the other had harassed a woman while he was drunk.[75]

Armies and Forced Prostitution

It is seldom a topic of discussion that armies have always enormously stimulated and still enormously stimulate the prostitution and forced prostitution industries. Indeed, they often first cause it to be produced and leave it behind after their withdrawal.[76] Japanese troops, soldiers in the German army, and African warlords have all forced women to be held as sex slaves for their soldiers "in order to keep them happy." A disastrous effect in terms of prostitution has been, for example, UN peacekeeping troops, who are not at all involved in combat operations.

At the beginning of the Vietnam War in 1957, there were an estimated 18,000 to 20,000 prostitutes. In 1953, and four military bases later, there were 400,000. Military bordellos were established under the supervision of generals. And it is no coincidence that the otherwise unattractive hotel and port city of Pattaya, where US soldiers spent their leave time, leaves Bangkok behind as a giant bordello. Everywhere that considerable numbers of soldiers were stationed, bordellos shot up like mushrooms. As a result, soldiers were not just clients. Rather, there were criminals among them who organized prostitution and forced prostitution or brought local prostitution under their control. This has been the case in Cambodia, Bosnia, and Kosovo.[77]

"Human rights organizations have seen that the stationing of UN troops has been the cause of a strong rise in the trafficking of women for forced prostitution in the respective regions. Thus, for example, Kosovo had become the main target for activities in trafficking women and girls, and the number of registered establishments in which women had to work

---

[75] „Obama: Sexuelle Übergriffe gefährden nationale Sicherheit" (translation of title: "Obama: Sexual attacks are undermining national security"), *Focus Online*, 17 May 2013. https://www.focus.de/politik/ausland/usa/sexattacken-beim-us-militaer-obama-missbrauch-gefaehrdet-nationale-sicherheit-_aid_992833.html.

[76] Most comprehensively documented in Barbara Drinck and Chung-Noh Gross (eds.), *Erzwungene Prostitution in Kriegs- und Friedenszeiten: Sexuelle Gewalt gegen Frauen und Mädchen* (translation of title: *Forced Prostitution in Times of War and Times of Peace: Sexual Violence against Women and Girls*; USP International, 2006).

[77] See Thomas Schirrmacher, *Human Trafficking: The Return to Slavery*, trans. Richard McClary (WEA Global Issues Series, vol. 12, 2013), 56f. https://iirf.eu/journal-books/global-issues-series/human-trafficking/

as forced prostitutes rose sharply since international peacekeeping forces (KFOR) were sent and the United Nations Interim Administrative Mission in Kosovo (UNMIK) was established. The situation has been aggravated due to the soldiers' immunity, which protects them from being prosecuted in court in the case of human rights violations."[78]

The Consequences of Rape

Psychological Consequences of Rape
Nightmares, sleep problems
Panic attacks, states of anxiety
Sexual disturbances and disturbances in relationships with sexual partners
Indifference, depression
Feelings of guilt
Self-harming behavior
Attempts to commit suicide; suicide

There are physical and psychological consequences to rape. Physical or bodily consequences are divided into direct consequences, such as bleeding, hematomas, and infections in the abdomen, but there are also consequences such as pregnancy or becoming infected with sexually transmitted diseases, all the way up to HIV and long-term consequences such as scars or infertility. According to the 2004 study commissioned by the German Ministry for Family Affairs mentioned above, the injuries suffered by victims include bruises (73%), vaginal injuries (32.7%), other internal injuries (5.4%), broken bones (2.3%), and miscarriages (3.5%).

Psychological (emotional) consequences are independent of whether there were no, slight, or severe physical injuries incurred and also arise if the victim was drugged during the rape. Often there are psychosomatic symptoms which arise in such cases, for instance, abdominal pain. During the crime, many victims experience mortal fear which can return later. Additionally, they can fall into a state of shock. The psychological consequences often continue for a long time. Most frequently, there are post-traumatic stress disorders. In time, a number of victims find their way back

---

[78]   http://www.ngo-online.de/lexikon/a-z/un-friedenstruppen-blauhelme.

into a normal way of life without being under care. Many achieve the same with the aid of counseling and support, though there are many who never get over the consequences, even into old age. Sometimes a relationship with someone who had been a partner up to that time does not survive, or women have difficulty becoming involved with a new partner.

Unquestionably exceptional victims are those women who become pregnant through rape in times of war. And the situation is not only on account of their own traumatization, which is frequently estimated to be as strong as that of victims of torture or of survivors of concentration camps. In many societies they find hardly any aid and support. Sometimes they are stigmatized as "offenders" or seen as complicit. Their children often carry this heavy burden into the next generation, such that the entire society is affected.

"If women become pregnant through rape during war, it is not only a society's present which is destroyed. Rather, it is also the future which is generated, with a generation of children procreated through rape and severely traumatized women. If women and girls survive what is often exceptionally brutal rape during wartime, the consequences usually overshadow their lives permanently. The effects are accurately compared with those of victims of torture and prisoners in concentration camps and classified according to the statistical manuals on psychological disorders (Diagnostic and Statistical Manual of Mental Disorders, or DSM, and the International Classification of Diseases, or ICD). Many victims of rape during war suffer from post-traumatic stress disorder. Along with that there are, for example, recurring and intrusive recollections, thoughts, perceptions, and dreams and physical and psychological stress when confronting certain stimuli which remind the individual of the rape. There are also flashback episodes. As a result, the victims frequently attempt to avoid thoughts, feelings, and conversations which are linked to the trauma and to avoid activities, places, and people that could evoke memories. That frequently means there is a drastic limitation on the quality of life. Many victims feel themselves alienated from other people and have the feeling of having a limited future. They may also show a limited spectrum of emotions. In addition, sleeping disorders often arise, as do difficulties concentrating, excessive vigilance, jumpiness. Depressive disorders, addiction and dependency, changes in personality, and dissociative disorders can be the consequences of rape during war times. . . . Comparative studies have analyzed that it is possible for realization to first come about with aging and as a consequence of the expectation of one's own death, when looking back on what has been experienced in one's life. To some extent, it can also come from looking back and realizing there have been forms of dissociative trauma. In this connection, there is a particular need for support for victims of rape in recent wars, all the way back to victims of rape during World War II."[79]

Even when wars or civil wars are over, women carry grave consequences. Whether it is a question of occupation or a long period of time until rule of law is restored, there is often very little which changes for these women. Even when the troops have finally pulled out, violence and discrimination may not end for these women. Although the women are completely innocent with respect to the rapes that occurred, they and the children they conceived are stigmatized or carry permanent diseases or handicaps. An additional consideration is the fact that women are practically never involved in peace negotiations and in political reconstruction (even the United Nations has never placed a woman in the position of chief peace negotiator). However, women often carry the major burden of restoring everyday life and the family – one just has to think of the Berlin "rubble women."

Forced Prostitution

Forced prostitution is a particularly difficult and permanent form of rape. Forced prostitutes can most closely be compared with slaves or bondwomen who must relinquish their right to self-determination to their "owner" (or pimp) and must surrender completely to their clients.

As a general rule, forced prostitutes "serve" 20 to 30 so-called clients per day during a period of work that lasts from 12 to 14 hours, without any free days or vacation. There are also many documented cases of longer work days and 60 to 70 clients per day. There is also no time off for illness, menstruation, or pregnancy. In addition, there are the consequences of abuse and food deprivation, as well as sexually transmitted diseases, and the consequences extend all the way to HIV/AIDS resulting from the failure to use a condom.

Whoever advocates equality for women but does not denounce the global trafficking of women and girls for purposes of prostitution loses all credibility. There is no other realm where women are more degraded and

[79] „Kriegsvergewaltigung – sexuelle Gewalt als Waffe" (translation of title: "Wartime rape: sexual violence as a weapon"), https://www.helpline-sh.de/vergewaltigung/kriegsvergewaltigung/.

delivered over to the power of men, and this in the middle of free, democratic states. Almost all countries on earth have strong legislation and punishments for rape, torture, and kidnapping. Forced prostitution comprises all three crimes simultaneously, but it is treated much more lackadaisically, is hardly investigated, and is lightly punished. And it must be made clear to the clients they are involved in such crimes.

To be very direct, the article on equality in the German Basic Law (Germany's constitution) on its own should be cause for enormously ramping up the battle against human trafficking and forced prostitution in Germany, making it one of the primary goals for the Federal Ministry of the Interior, the Federal Ministry of Labor and Social Affairs, and the Federal Ministry for Family Affairs. There is nothing which places equality into question more than the fact that every day millions of men pay for a businesslike, arranged rape, and that for a few euros they buy the right to treat women as they wish or as they have seen on the internet or in films, to humiliate them, and to intimidate them. From what little the German government does, one might believe there is almost no forced prostitution in Germany. Detlef Ubben is the head of the department addressing issues related to human trafficking with the Hamburg State Criminal Police Office. He estimates that "95% of prostitutes are forced prostitutes." What does that mean? Ubben states: "These women do not work for their own account and are not based on self-determination. If they refuse, a violent scene ensues." The women are left with only 10% of their wages.[80]

In a number of Asian countries such as Japan, China, Korea, and Taiwan, sex with a virgin is seen as the ultimate experience and is supposed to bring luck and commercial success. (The fear of contracting AIDS also plays a part.) Often the same girls are sold as "virgins" multiple times. For that reason, rich "clients" often buy girls directly from parents. There are documented cases in which wealthy Japanese or Chinese pay the means of subsistence from the time of the birth of a girl to penniless Asian parents in order to be able to then take her as a virgin one day. (In internet pornography, women are frequently offered as virgins for their alleged first sexual contact. The high demand for such "offers" speaks for itself.)

---

[80]   „95 Prozent sind Opfer: Für Hauptkommissar Detlev Ubben entspricht die Unterscheidung zwischen Prostitution und Zwangsprostitution nicht der Realität" (translation of title: "95 per cent are victims: according to police commissioner Detlev Ubben the distinction between prostitution and compelled prostitution does not correspond to the reality"), https://www.emma.de/artikel/hamburger-kommissar-95-prozent-sind-opfer-263727.

Wole Soyinka, the African Nobel Prize winner for literature, mentions the system in Ghana exposed by the CNN journalist Christiana Amanpour as an example of slavery, according to which a girl lives as a slave of a priest because she is a bride of the gods. She must do this until she is no longer beautiful. The priest owes her nothing, and she owes the priest everything. Rape is the general rule.[81]

Violent Pornography

At this point, violent pornography, found above all on the internet, must be mentioned. Violent pornography is theoretically forbidden in Germany. We will not take up the topic in great detail in English as we have done in German.[82] Unfortunately, it is still a taboo subject that the message contained in such pornography, that a woman is available to fulfil any "desires," destroys all the successes of equality without any protest. Even where feminist professors have demonstrated a connection between this type of pornography and the murder of women, they are in danger of standing there and appearing to be "conservative" or "living in the past" and of easily being catapulted into a situation where they are socially marginalized because of such statements.[83] A social outcry should be provoked solely because of the fact that these images most often arise through violence committed against real women.

Recently, one of the authors was on a rather sensationally presented television program. Called "One-on-One," it was aired by the German broadcaster Sat 1. In the program, two male professors lined up against two known porn stars to discuss whether a heightened consumption of pornography changes our behavior. In my disapprobation, I zeroed in on depictions of rape on the internet. Even with this point, both porn stars were unable to be moved to say anything negative about pornography. They maintained that it only had to do with performances and fantasies. Also, the person whom it is satisfying should just be allowed to have his fun. In their view, we were men who only wanted to forbid women from

---

[81]   Wole Soyinka, „Kulturelle Ansprüche und globale Rechte," (translatio of title: "Cultural claims and global rights"), in *Versprochen - Verletzt - Gefordert: 50 Jahre Allgemeine Erklärung der Menschenrechte* (Bonn: Forum Menschenrechte Materialien, vol. 12, 1998), 45-46.

[82]   See Thomas Schirrmacher, *Internetpornografie* (SCM Hänssler, 2008).

[83]   See Diana E. H. Russell, "Femicidal Pornography," 50-60 in Diana E. H. Russell and Roberta A. Ahrmes (eds.), *Femicide in Global Perspective* (New York: Teachers College Press, 2001).

having fun. What an upside-down world: A sociologist and a sexual scientist were combating the glorification of sexualized violence, and two women were defending it![84] The statement we made at that time was only confirmed through all of this: "The depiction of violent pornography against women reverses all achievements of equality. Women become undignified objects, and their 'no' becomes foreplay. And yet the feminist movement continues to be right: In the case of rape and its depiction, it is not a matter of sex but rather of violence and power and domination over women. In contrast, we need a consensus in society as a whole, above all that we do not seek to burn this undignified view of women into the minds of children and adolescents."

The psychologist Herbert Selg, who is himself an advocate of pornography, has researched the resultant psychological problems of pornography on behalf of the pornographic magazine *Penthouse* and summarized them pointedly in 1986: "Erotica frequently has male models endowed with especially impressive genitals and outstanding potency. It is probable that what are already widespread male feelings of inferiority are thereby fortified. … If you address clinical psychologists and doctors regarding pornography, they complain about the pressure to perform which arises from the extreme depictions found in works of pornography. Women are correspondingly depicted in a distorted manner. For starters, only models are chosen who are predominantly attuned to the present ideal of beauty as held by the class of consumers addressed. As a result, there are many photographic 'supplements' which are possible so that in the final event almost flawless and youthful bodies are offered. … Furthermore, pornographic material portrays the behavior and experiences of women according to the desires of the men involved in its production: partners who are always sexually responsive – or as sex objects who are readily available. Men either intentionally or unintentionally compare their partners in everyday life to porn models. This can lead to perverse expectations with respect to female attractiveness and sexual willingness."[85]

Hard pornography and internet pornography make many consumers aggressive – above all with respect to women – and, more specifically, it increases existing aggression, since pornography is often not the sole cause of such aggression. When violence is joined with the depiction of

---

[84] http://www.sat1.de/tv/eins-gegen-eins/episoden/thema-porno-als-massenphae nomen-macht-das-unsere-gesellschaft-kaputt; comp. http://www.thomasschirr macher.info/archives/2097.

[85] Herbert Selg, *Pornographie: Psychologische Beiträge zur Wirkungsforschung* (Bern: Verlag Hans Huber, 1986), 76-77.

sexual acts, this effect on aggression applies to a greater degree. Many studies have shown that under certain circumstances, pornography promotes aggressive behavior.[86] As a general rule, if people who are already aggressive are shown pornographic material, their aggression increases. Sex and violence in "normal" motion pictures increase the willingness and the desire to use violence against women, and that is the case with or without sexual acts. Diane E.H. Russell points to Neil Malamuth's report for the US Attorney General, where a study has shown that 10 percent of male students were aroused by pornography with extreme violence and blood and limited sexual elements, 20-30 percent by films in which the woman only demonstrated refusal and no consent, and 50-60 percent if the victim of rape indeed consented in the end.

Hard pornography with or without violence increases the willingness to commit rape on the part of men who admit to already being so inclined, as many studies have shown. In particular, it brings forth the "rape myth" or amplifies it. The English term "rape myth" was coined, described as to its content, and documented by Martha R. Burt in 1980. What does "rape mythology" say? In brief: Women who are raped find pleasure in it in the end. We find a good presentation of this by psychologist Herbert Selg, who described the rape myth on behalf of the pornographic magazine *Penthouse*.

The Rape Myth says the following:
Regarding the victims/women:
"(1) All women (actually) want to be raped. They enjoy acts of rape.
(2) No woman can be raped against her will. Only bad women are raped or rather can be raped.
(3a) Women wrongfully accuse a man of rape, for example, when he wants to ditch them.
(3b) Women wrongfully accuse a man if they have something else to hide (for example, if they are caught in the act when having an affair)."
Regarding the offenders/men:
"(1) Men who commit rape are ill.
(2a) Men who commit rape are sex-starved.

---

[86]   Listed and discussed in Schirrmacher, *Internetpornografie*.

> (2b) Men who commit rape have such a strong sex drive that they can hardly do otherwise.
>
> The function of such theses is clear: They excuse the offender and blame the victim."[87]

Sexist Advertising with Women as Structural Violence

Advertising which is sexist toward women can itself be interpreted as violence against women. When scantily dressed, thin, young women with perfect looks are utilized to heighten the attention paid to a product and to increase its sales, from the point of view of women's rights activists, this is not only an illusion but rather a degradation of women.

"Advertising passes on social role models and demonstrates how women and men allegedly have to be. Children are shaped by these images early on. In particular, the presentation of scantily clad women is readily used in order to draw attention to a product which, on the basis of its content, most often has no connection to the female body. Using the motto 'sex sells,' the aid provided, in part, by pornographic depictions is supposed to sell electronics, cars, and other products and even generate donations for charities or relief organizations. However, it is not only the reduction of the female body to a sexual object that is a form of discrimination. Rather, it is a clichéd depiction of both women and men. It perpetuates sex or gender roles, reinforces prejudices and fortifies a hetero-normative standard. This societal normalization can be felt by individuals as a form of violence – particularly when linked to abasement and marginalization and when certain power structures are reinforced. For example, the nonappearance of other examples of roles and the failure to depict other sexual identities illustrates a form of marginalization. A degradation takes place, for example, when the female body is presented as a product which is available anytime, an object which poses naked or scantily clad in front of a camera, and in the process uses provocative body language to declare that women can be bought and are sexy. Sexist advertising means women are reduced to their beauty, explicitly related to certain body parts. According to the way women are represented in advertising,

---

[87]   Herbert Selg, *Pornographie* 93, 94.

socially latent and omnipresent sexism is especially clear: Sexist advertising presupposes male dominance, heterosexuality, and a dualistic gender theory as the social norm."[88]

Female Genital Mutilation

Female genital mutilation (FGM) is often referred to as "female circumcision" as a way to downplay it. It belongs to one of the darkest chapters of the oppression of women. "UNICEF estimates that currently more than 200 million women and girls in 30 countries have been genitally mutilated. However, this number can only be understood as a rough estimate, as precise prevalence studies currently still do not exist for many countries. The actual rate could therefore be up to twice as high. . . . Also in Germany, women and girls are exposed to the risk of being genitally mutilated secretly inside the country, or taken abroad and forced to undergo the procedure," writes Terre des Femmes.[89]

Presumably, this gruesome practice of removing a part or all of the outer genitals (clitoris and / or labia minora and labia majora) and of sewing up the vagina to leave only a small opening, stems from Africa, where this practice is supposed to have already been practiced since the time of the pharaohs. With the emergence of Islam, the practice remained in several African cultures to the present day and is mostly justified by the necessity of maintaining the women's virginity. Over 90 percent of the girls in Egypt, (North) Sudan, Mali, Somalia, Guinea, and Sierra Leone are circumcised.[90] The notion that this procedure is necessary is so generally widespread that girls would otherwise hardly have a chance to get married; in such case, they are ridiculed, marginalized, and their parents are placed under enormous social pressure. If a mother still wants to safeguard her daughter from circumcision, girls are often abducted and are forcibly subjected to circumcision.

---

[88] http://frauenrechte.de/online/index.php/themen/frauenfeindliche-werbung.html. Comp. the excellent „Checkliste frauenfeindlicher Werbung" (translation of title: "Check list of misogynistic advertising") with convincing examples of advertising at https://www.frauenrechte.de/online/index.php/themen-und-aktionen/frauenfeindliche-werbung/checkliste.

[89] "Female Genital Mutilation," https://frauenrechte.de/online/index.php/en/our-work/focus-areas/female-genital-mutilation-fgm.

[90] The best overview is offered in the chart in Seager, *Atlas of Women*, 53-55.

Mutilation is predominately conducted under extremely primitive medical conditions and without anesthesia, and it results in numerous fatalities on an annual basis; the number of victims who fight their entire life with complications and who are traumatized victims of this gruesome maltreatment cannot even be estimated. The World Health Organization (WHO) assumes a number of around 100 million circumcised girls and women who are over the age of ten. FGM has also come to Europe through migration; girls from several African countries are subject to this ritual by circumcisers who are flown in or through visits to their home countries. The number of affected or endangered girls in Germany is estimated to be 30,000.

The Arabellion in Egypt has not led to a situation where genital mutilation has been totally rejected and is being reduced in the name of women's human rights. The situation is mixed. Some Islamic authorities have sought its renewed legalization. While the United Nations passed a resolution against FGM on December 20, 2012, theologians in Egypt play down this practice. Many theologians themselves say the practice is not prescribed by Islam. And some Muslim authorities in Egypt even call it a crime now.[91]

Possible consequences of female genital mutilation
Reduced ability to experience sexual arousal
Pain during sexual activity and when urinating
Susceptibility to infection in the lower abdomen
Cysts in the lower abdomen
Infertility
Complications during birth and an increased risk of miscarriages
Necessary follow-up operations
Death

Household Slavery

Household slavery is an additional area where women are oppressed. These women are underpaid or not paid at all in many countries. They

---

91 "Female genital mutilation is forbidden in Islam: Dar Al-Ifta," http://www.egypt independent.com/female-genital-mutilation-is-not-islamic-dar-al-ifta-says/.

have to grind away without pay for many hours per day. Frequently they do not have legal documents or visas, do not have health insurance, and are subject to assault by their employers. They often are not able to effectively defend themselves against their employers and, because of their lack of rights, are completely at their mercy. They are subject to arbitrary treatment if their employers retain their papers. In many cases, these women and girls are sexually exploited. The International Labor Association estimates that more than 9,000,000 women and girls were household slaves in 2016.[92]

The *Neue Züricher Zeitung* (a Swiss daily newspaper published in Zurich) has written about the situation in Europe in connection with a resolution by the parliamentary assembly of the European Council: "As far as the victims are concerned, it primarily has to do with women who are employed in private households, au pair girls or so-called catalogue wives. Most of them initially leave home by their own free will because they want to escape the poverty and misery in their countries of origin. Others reach Europe by being deceived by their employer or by agencies, by becoming ensnared in debt, or by just being downright sold. Once they have taken up their work or have married a man appearing to be a client, they are dependent and isolated. They are degraded to slaves – it is not an exception for them to have to work up to 18 hours per day in the household without their own room and without any medical care. In particular, one finds that these destinies are the brutal reality in the diplomatic environment and are everything but isolated cases."[93]

The International Society for Human Rights, for example, reports with respect to Lebanon: "There are Asian and African household helpers who slave away for $100-$200 per month in over 100,000 households in Lebanon. Their legal situation is precarious, and abuse is not infrequent. The problem for women is that they are illegal as soon as they leave the family with whom they are under contract. Their residence permit is tied to their employment contract. 'If a woman runs away from her employer, she no longer has a residence permit,' Roukoss explains. In addition, the employer retains the woman's identification papers as a form of security. According

---

[92] Global Estimates of Modern Slavery, 2016. http://www.ilo.org/wcmsp5/groups/public/---dgreports/---dcomm/documents/publication/wcms_575479.pdf.

[93] „Haushaltssklaven in Europa: Bericht des Europarats über Menschenrechtsverletzungen" (translation of title: "Household slaves in Europe: A Report of the Council of Europe regarding Human Rights Violations"), *Neue Zürcher Zeitung* 24 June, 2004, p. 17.

to a 2005 survey by Caritas, 90 percent of Lebanese families with maids operate based on this pattern. Thus, women are de facto at the mercy of their employers. This uncertain situation on the part of women makes them particularly vulnerable to human rights violations. Seventy-one percent of Lebanese who hire household help are of the opinion that they are able to limit the freedom of movement of the women. Indeed, only two percent of those asked indicated that they have the right to physically punish their maid. However, in the same survey, 31 percent indicated that they still hit their female household help when they do not follow their directions."[94]

Trafficking in Women

There is a separate volume in this series which addresses the topic of human trafficking and is entitled *Human Trafficking*.[95] The topic can only be sketched here. Up to 80 percent of all people affected by human trafficking are female. Women can more flexibly be used as "merchandise," can be more readily kept in check through force, and because of their lower status in their countries of origin, are more likely to be sold to human traffickers. In addition, when it comes to forced prostitution, girls and women are more in demand for heterosexual contact than boys for homosexual contact.

According to the website of the United Nations' global office responsible for capturing criminal activity, the United Nations Office on Drugs and Crime (UNODC), about 80 percent of the victims of human trafficking land in forced prostitution. Seventy-nine percent of the victims of human trafficking are girls.

The United Nations' International Organization for Migration (IOM), based in Geneva, estimates that annually about 500,000 women and children are trafficked from Eastern and Central Europe to Western Europe.

Despite these statistics, the public shows little interest in the topic. When the television moderator Michel Friedman was caught in flagrante delicto with several prostitutes from Ukraine in 2003, in the course of criminal investigations against trafficking in women, his consumption of cocaine caused a greater stir than the fact that a criminal organization had

---

94 Björn Zimprich, „Maids sind ein Statussymbol" (translation of title: "Maids are a Status Symbol"), Internationale Gesellschaft für Menschenrechte, May, 2011. https://www.igfm.de/themen/frauenrechte/libanon-maids/.

95 Thomas Schirrmacher, *Human Trafficking: The Return of Slavery* (Bonn, Germany: Culture and Science Pub., 2013). https://www.bucer.de/ressource/details/hu man-trafficking.html.

supplied him with women by force. Friedman apologized before the public, his friends, and many other people. Yet he never publicly apologized to the forced prostitutes despite being called upon to do so.[96]

Even the fact that human trafficking often finances terrorism appears to raise little interest. The Taliban have their own women wear veils but traffic girls and women from other people groups or give away women as thanks to deserving combatants. The Turkish PKK and the Near Eastern Hezbollah also finance their terrorist activities through drug dealing and human trafficking. One leader of the Islamic Hezbollah in a prison in Vienna ran a human trafficking ring via his cell phone. Even his henchmen had no idea for whom they were generating cash.

A particularly underhanded way of exploiting women is their use in so-called flat rate bordellos: "'Sex with all the women you want, as long as you want, as often as you want, and how you want it' – this is the way the chain of brothels called the 'Pussy Club' advertised its locations for so-called flat rate sex in Fellbach (near Stuttgart), Heidelberg, Berlin, and Wuppertal. Beginning on . . ., pimps for these brothels have to answer to the Stuttgart regional court's 10th Larger Court Division for Business Offences. . . . Since 2004, the ten defendants are supposed to have regularly brought young Romanians to Germany in order to have them work under their control as prostitutes. . . . The 22 Romanian women who became the victims of the human trafficking ring came to Germany to earn money. 'Earning money' means, however, serving up to 60 tricks in what are up to 14-hour days – indeed, none of the women expected this. Many of the women were not even 21 years old at the time. . . . 'On weekends there were more guys standing in front of the door of the Fellbach Pussy Club than in front of the best discos in Stuttgart,' stated attorney Jens Rabe from Waiblingen. . . . There were times when a woman did not allow just anything to be done to her, although the chain of brothels promised that to their clients. If a guest complained about this, the prostitutes' weekly salary was eliminated. The women's salaries reportedly range from €350 to €1,000."[97]

[96] Lea Ackerman, Inga Bell, and Barbara Koelges, *Verkauft, versklavt, zum Sex gez-wungen* (translation of title: *Sold, Enslaved, and Compelled to have Sex*; Kösel-Verlag, 2005), 73.

[97] Judith Kubitscheck, „Flatrate-Bordell-Zuhälter müssen vor Gericht," in: *Die Welt* (a German Newspaper), 7 March 2011. https://www.welt.de/vermischtes/weltge schehen/article12724908/Flatrate-Bordell-Zuhaelter-muessen-vor-Gericht.html.

Forced Marriage

Marriages where women possess no right to a say and where, instead of negotiating *with* them, they are negotiated *about,* represent a particularly serious violation of human rights and an especially serious form of coercion. If a marriage comes about, continuous rape comes with it.

Forced marriage today is particularly well-known in Muslim-majority countries, above all in the Near East and in South Asia (e.g., Pakistan, Afghanistan) and has also become a problem in Western countries through migration. However, arranged and forced marriages were and are a known phenomenon in cultures characterized by Christianity, Judaism, and Hinduism. It is also practiced in Buddhist and Yazidi cultures. For a long time, arranged marriages were a widespread practice among members of the nobility and within the upper educated classes. One finds marriages arranged by parents in the Near East in population groups characterized by both Christianity and Islam. The border between an arranged marriage and a forced marriage is frequently fluid, namely at that point when the initiative to conclude a marriage originates from the family and the agreement of the involved individual is not only expected but where there is hardly a chance of rejecting the family's plans. It is clearly a question of forced marriage in each case where the participants unmistakably reject the marriage, are coerced by force to conclude the marriage, or as children are unable to decide for themselves.

It is not only cultures characterized by patriarchy, and the demand for obedience by women to Sharia law in the Near East and in South Asia, which contribute to the continuation of forced marriages. It is also not the tradition which grants a right of determination over the woman to the father, grandfather, brother, or uncle. Rather, it is a society marked by collective thinking which only slightly considers individual wishes. There is in these societies a notion of honor in which the behavior of the woman (especially when she rejects the chosen marital candidate or expresses her own marital desires) endangers or destroys the honor of the man – and thus his social reputation and that of the entire family.

Indeed, according to Sharia law provisions, the bride is to be asked for her consent to the marriage. However, Sharia law also determines that a woman is supposed to be obedient to her father or husband. Traditionally, it has been the family of the bridegroom who initiates the marriage, and it is the family of the bride who then agrees (an independent search by a bride for a marital candidate is, within this traditional framework, not envisaged). Thus, under certain circumstances, the parents go over the heads of the bridal couple and agree without the bridal couple having a real opportunity to oppose the marriage, let alone permitting them to go out on their own in search of a partner. Additionally, women in many Muslim-majority countries have a limited legal capacity and require the agreement of a guardian for the conclusion of a marital contract. Thus, a marriage can hardly be entered without the consent of a male relative. In countries characterized by Islam but which are officially secular, such as Turkey and Indonesia, women have better options.

On the positive side, the phenomenon of forced marriage is today receiving more attention around the world. Forced marriage was recognized as a violation of human rights for the first time at the UN World Conference in 2000 in Bejing.[98] A number of Muslim-majority countries have passed laws against forced marriage, Turkey, for example, though passing a law does not guarantee the law's implementation and the eradication of forced marriage. In Germany, forced marriages have been taken up in Section 237 of the Penal Code as its own criminal offence within the criminal code.[99]

Reliable nationwide statistics for Germany on the number of arranged marriages or on the number of forced marriages in Western countries do not exist; in individual cities, such as Berlin or Hamburg, there are, however, several hundred documented cases per year. According to the opinion of human rights and women's rights activists, it is possible that a high number of unreported cases should be added to this figure. There have been several studies of the problem. Those conducted on behalf of the Berlin Senate Administration and the Federal Ministry for Family Affairs, Senior Citizens, Women, and Youth collected data from 1,500 counseling centers and 3,443 individuals who sought help.[100] Of those people, some 60 percent turned to the counseling centers because of forced marriages. The estimates for the number of forced marriages fluctuates between 10 per-

---

[98] According to Silvia Tellenbach, „Ehen wider Willen: Anmerkungen zur Zwangs-verheiratung in Deutschland" (translation of title: "Marriage against one will: observation about compelled marriages in Germany"), in Sabih Arkan and Firat Öz-tan, *Prof. Dr. Fırat Öztan'a armağan. II. Cilt* (Ankara: Turhan Kitabevi, 2010), 2037-2052, here 2038.

[99] Until then § 240 Par. 4.1 saw forced marriage as a "particularly severe case" of coercion.

[100] Bundesministeriums für Familie, Senioren, Frauen und Jugend, *Zwangsverheira-tung in Deutschland* (translation of title: *Forced Marriage in Germany*; Baden-Baden: Nomos, 2011).

cent, when looking at all marriages where there is a migration background, and 50 percent, when considering all female Turks entering Germany.[101] The number of men forced to marry has nowhere been compiled.

Motives for individuals participating in forced marriages
Financial and material interests, for example, a bride price, dowry, or inheritance
Sons and daughters in Western countries should marry a partner from areas from which they come or with the religion or culture from which they come to prevent westernization (e.g., those individuals of Turkish origin in Germany receive a wife from Anatolia).
Family fears of the loss of "honor," for example, because of the possible loss of virginity
Obtaining residence permits in an EU or Western country
Combating homosexuality, i.e., children who have homosexual or lesbian feelings are married off, and children are to be protected from such feelings

A particular form of forced marriage is "girl theft." This occurs in individual cases where Islamists in Egypt kidnap girls who are Coptic Christians and marry them to mostly older Muslim men. An alternative way this form of forced marriage frequently occurs is that after a war, the girls from the opponent's side are carried off and forced to marry.

Child Marriage

In many parts of the world, child marriage is practiced, especially among poorer, rural population groups of a traditional nature.[102] UN Women estimates that annually there are 60 million girls around the world under the age of 18 who are married as child brides. Of that number, 31.1 million are in South Asia and 14.1 million in sub-Saharan Africa.

Poverty is often a motive, if, for example, the parents either are glad to no longer have to care for the daughter or the entire family profits from the marriage and, in a certain sense, the child sacrifices herself for the family. Prostitution would be a worse alternative.

---

[101] Ibid.
[102] Numbers and chart in Seager, *Atlas*, 24.

In Muslim-majority societies, worrying about the good reputation of the family also arises in addition to the problematic aspects of poverty, whereby the virginity of the daughter has to be preserved. Additionally, there is the fact that, according to texts held to be binding, Mohammed, who is the central role model for Muslims, entered into a very early marriage with his favorite wife, Aisha. A number of texts from tradition speak of Aisha only being nine years old at the time of the marriage. It is difficult for Muslims to truly rescind this, because, in the opinion of many theologians, Mohammed has the position of an indisputable role model. Many Orthodox Islamic theologians have advocated the fundamental possibility of very early marriages. Other theologians believe Aisha would have been 16 or 17 years of age at the time of her marriage to Mohammed; others who are more progressive in their thinking hold that one must make adjustments befitting the social circumstances.

Some Muslim-majority countries have raised the minimum marrying age in recent decades. Tunisia raised the minimum marrying age to 15 in 1956 and to 17 in 1964. In 2007, the minimum marrying age was adjusted to that of men and raised to 18. According to UN Women and UNICEF, the portion of individuals marrying under 20 years of age dropped from 50 percent in 1960 to 3 percent in 2004.[103]

Legislation alone is not effective in protecting against early marriages when a traditional rural environment and limited educational opportunities and decision-making choices go hand-in-hand with poverty and patriarchalism. In line with this situation, there was a 2008 case which made its way into public awareness. In that case, a Yemeni girl who was then eight years old was able to push through a divorce from her husband, 22 years her elder, whom she had been forced to marry. However, she had to pay a large amount of compensation to her husband.[104] There are repeated cases of marriage between men with young girls which become public knowledge in Gulf Region countries, including Saudi Arabia. There is significant health risk to young mothers and their babies where kinship is too close, including an increased risk of handicaps.

Although it is legally forbidden in South Asia, child marriage remains widespread, especially in rural areas. The abolishment of child marriage has been a concern for many Indian social reformers, such as Ram Mohan Roy, Ishwar Chandra Vidyasagar, and Mahatma Gandhi. In 1929 the Child

---

[103] UN Women, *Progress of the World's Women: In Pursuit of Justice* (2011), 29. http://www.unwomen.org/en/digital-library/publications/2011/7/progress-of-the-world-s-women-in-pursuit-of-justice.

[104] "Nujood Ali," https://en.wikipedia.org/wiki/Nujood_Ali.

Marriage Restraint Act was passed into law, prescribing a marrying age of at least 18 for girls and 21 for boys. According to information provided by the *Rapid Household Survey*, which was conducted in all of India, in the state of Bihar, 58.9 percent of girls were married prior to their reaching their 18th birthday, while in the states of Rajasthan and in West Bengal, the percentages were about 55 percent.[105]

Honor Killings

Admittedly, honor killings have no basis in Islamic theology. The Koran does not comment on the topic of honor killings, and even less does it mandate them. Nevertheless, honor killings take place primarily in societies shaped by Islam. Here, particularly in rural, traditional areas, norms for husband and wife are strictly defined and grounded in religious decrees that are collectively monitored. Additionally, violations are, above all, blamed on women. Women are the first victims when punishment is meted out, mostly through their being deprived of freedom. In the most extreme cases, they become the victims of honor killings.

Early in 2005, a young woman of Turkish descent met her death in this manner in the middle of Berlin. Hatun Sürücü's family had charged her with living alone, "like a German." She was killed at the hands of her brother in broad daylight – for reasons of "honor." There are several such officially known cases in Germany; around the world, there are supposedly approximately 5,000 such cases annually, though the number of unreported cases may be significantly higher. Traditional tribal societal norms are a basis, as is the rigid observation of traditions, some of which reflect the desire to "protect" one's family and its honor. The room women have for decision-making and self-determination is severely restricted. In the case of violations because of too many "freedoms" the woman allows herself, she can be punished through force or even killed by her own family. There are also instances of male victims of honor killings when they commit extreme violations against culturally and religiously defined norms (e.g., when their homosexuality is revealed).

A study of honor killings conducted on behalf of the Federal Criminal Police Office examined all case files and media reports of honor killings reported in Germany from 1996 to 2005.[106] According to this study, of the

---

[105] http://de.wikipedia.org/wiki/Kinderheirat (May 17, 2013), verified in the sources. See also https://en.wikipedia.org/wiki/Child_marriage.

[106] Dietrich Oberwittler and Julia Kasselt, „Ehrenmorde in Deutschland 1996-2005" (translation of title: "Honor Murders in Germany 1996-2005," Freiburg in Breisgau:

122 offenders, 93 percent, or 103, were male and 9 were female. Of the victims, 47 (43 percent) were male and 62 (57 percent) were female. That corresponds with studies in Turkey, which show that offenders are predominantly men while the victims are often in equal measure men and women.

Honor killings are mostly disguised as accidents or suicide, even in Germany which follows the rule of law. Naturally, in countries where the public or even the judiciary endorses honor killings, this is easier. On the positive side, honor killings and forced marriages are receiving more attention today, and some institutions are offering assistance to those affected.

A special form of honor killings is dowry death. The regional information center of the UN for Western Europe (UNRIC) explains: "One speaks of dowry death when a wife is killed by her husband or her parents-in-law because the bride cannot fulfill the dowry expectations. The dowry is a payment which the family of the woman is expected to make to the man's family as a gift at the time of the engagement or at the time of the wedding. It is common for the dowry to exceed the annual income of an entire family. The dowry or a similar payment is found in many cultures around the world. Killings because of an insufficient dowry payment primarily occur in South Asia."[107] According to news reports, there are more than 20 women killed every day in India in connection with disputes over dowries.[108]

Stoning

According to traditional Islamic criminal law, stoning is the proper sanction for married adulterers, male or female. According to most legal scholars, however, conditions require four male eyewitnesses or a confession by the accused. These conditions can almost never be fulfilled. Some theologians believe that a victim of stoning should be given the opportunity to

---

The Max Planck Institute for Foreign and International Criminal Law, 2010). https://www.mpicc.de/de/forschung/forschungsarbeit/kriminologie/ehrenmor de.html.

[107] „Gewalt gegen Frauen weltweit," (translation of title: "Violence against Women Worldwide") https://www.unric.org/de/frauen-pressemitteilungen/4861.

[108] Chayyanika Nigam, "21 lives lost to dowry every day across India; conviction rate less than 35 per cent," *India Today*, April 22, 2017. https://www.indiatoday.in/ mail-today/story/dowry-deaths-national-crime-records-bureau-conviction-rate-972874-2017-04-22.

flee. However, Sharia criminal law is not in force even in most Muslim-majority countries.

Exceptions, however, are found in the cases of a few countries such as Iran, which reintroduced the Sharia as the comprehensive legal and legislative foundation after the 1979 Islamic Revolution. Another is Saudi Arabia, which does not have a codified penal code and has judges administer justice solely according to the Koran and tradition (Arabic: Sunna).

Under the Western-oriented Shah regime, women received all political rights in Iran in 1963. In 1967, the final Sharia laws for family law were removed. Women received access to all professions and state offices. The percentage of women at university in Iran during the 1970s counted among the highest in the world. In 1979, all such legal and practical forms of progress were eliminated. Not only were all women again legally subordinated to men. Stoning was also reintroduced. And when it comes to adultery, it is typically the case that almost always only the women are stoned and not the men involved.[109]

According to information available from the International Society for Human Rights, official sentences of stoning and stoning without sentencing have been practiced in recent years in Afghanistan, Iran, Iraq, Yemen, Nigeria, Pakistan, Saudi Arabia, Somalia, Sudan, and the United Arab Emirates, not to mention individual cases in some other countries where stoning is not typical. Stoning is found in the penal codes of Saudi Arabia, the United Arab Emirates, Pakistan, Sudan, Iran, and Yemen, as well as in the Northern states of Nigeria. In addition, it is in the penal code in other countries even where it is not administered.

The Pew Research Center collects data on the relationship between religion and society around the world. It has published the results of a survey regarding severe corporal punishment in six significant countries where the majority of the population is Muslim. According to the research, 82 percent of the population in Egypt and Pakistan, 70 percent of the population in Jordan, and 56 percent of the population in Nigeria advocate stoning. In what is comparatively tolerant Indonesia, the level is still 42 percent.[110]

"Stoning is the cruelest and most painful method of execution. The victim is wrapped in linen towels, buried up to the chest in a hole in the

---

[109] Ockrent, *Schwarzbuch*, 104-116.
[110] "Muslim Publics Divided on Hamas and Hezbollah," Pew Research Center, December 2, 2010. http://www.pewglobal.org/2010/12/02/muslims-around-the-world-divided-on-hamas-and-hezbollah/.

ground, and then stoned. The stones inflict serious injuries to the condemned individual, but they are not enough to kill him or her immediately.
The victims die slowly and torturously. Stoning is a cruel, inhumane, and
demeaning punishment in the sense of the United Nations Convention
against Torture and Other Cruel, Inhuman, or Degrading Treatment or
Punishment ... In Iran there have been numerous executions of this type
in recent years. There are repeatedly new sentences of stoning, which,
above all, are handed down on account of adultery. Most victims are
women. Reasons for this are discrimination against women and fundamen-
talists' laws which are sexist toward women. According to the law, women
in Iran do not have the same rights as men and are not treated equally in
court. When women come into contact with the law, they are usually ar-
rested and interrogated by men. It is exclusively men who pass judgment
with respect to them. Women are often forced to give confessions through
torture. Women are the victims of unfair court proceedings in rural areas
because they cannot read and write, and for that reason they confess to
crimes which they did not even commit. In many cases, women who be-
longed to ethnic minorities do not speak Persian, the official legal language. They do not understand what is happening to them in a court proceeding or even that a stoning is a threat for them. According to
fundamentalist laws, the judge can render a sentence of stoning solely according to his own subjective discretion. Most women who are charged are
not able to afford good legal counsel."[111]

Gendercide – the Murder of Women

"Gendercide," a word originated in 1985 by Mary Anne Warren, has become a new word combining the concepts of gender and genocide and des-
ignating the systematic and massive-scale killing of members of a gender
on account of gender. If one wants to limit the term to women, one can use
the term femicide, known in English since about 1800 and which Diana E.
H. Russell introduced as a technical term into the academic discussion. The
systematic killing of men is only found in war and after a war, which is
undertaken to decimate a country's military strength.[112] Femicide includes
all massive killing of women, indeed every murder of a woman or a girl,
when it happens because she is female. The term has occasionally been

---

[111] http://www.menschenrechtsverein.org/index.php/cat/18/title/Stoppt%20die%
       20Steinigungen!
[112] Case studies at http://www.gendercide.org/case.html.

extended to also include all murders of women, for instance, those also committed by women. This, however, does not appear sensible to us.

Many serial killers are killers of women. Jack the Ripper is, unfortunately, a sad reality up to the present day. The few women who are serial killers mostly kill women. This also applies to so-called "angels of death" in hospitals, who mostly kill older women.

In the Mexican city of Ciudad Juárez, which lies across from the Texan city of El Paso, the local situation is known to us because of a large humanitarian project. The Organization of American States Inter-American Commission on Human Rights as well as the human rights organization The Dead Women of Juárez, as it is called, have investigated this situation in the city and the neighboring city of Chihuahua in detail. For a period of time up to 2005, there were 370 documented murders of women between the ages of 12 and 22. For a long time, these women were counted as missing and had been either unloaded in the desert or in uninhabited areas; one-third of them were raped and practically all had been tortured, tormented, and disfigured. Additionally, there were hundreds of girls counted as missing. In 2010, a total of 270 such murders of women were reported for the surrounding state of Chihuahua, 247 of which were directly in Juárez. The numbers for 2011 and 2012 were similarly high.[113]

One-third of all women who are killed annually in the USA are killed by friends, intimate partners, life companions, ex-husbands, and husbands. In South Africa, a woman is killed by a partner every six hours.

Gendercide – Gender Selection through Abortion

The term gendercide or femicide is often used to designate a particular form of killing of members of the female gender, namely gender-specific abortion or the forced abortion of girls.[114] This occurs in countries or cultures where great value is placed on male descendants, primarily in China, India, and South Korea. This has been strengthened in China by the one-child policy – if only one child is allowed, then it should be a boy. In India, poverty plays a large role since boys determine how the family will be provided for. Girls, on the other hand, can mean there is a high cost for a

---

[113] Thoroughly investigated in the collective volume: Alicia Gaspar de Alba, among others (eds.), *Making a Killing: Femicide, Free Trade, and La Frontera* (Austin: University of Texas Press, 2010); summary in Ockrent, *Schwarzbuch*, 117-131. Also see http://www.feministezine.com/feminist/international/Gender-Violence-in-Me xico.html.

[114] On prenatal diagnosis see Ute Buth and Thomas Schirrmacher, *Schwangerschaftsabbruch: Fakten und Entscheidungshilfen* (Holzgerlingen: SCM Hänssler, 2013).

dowry. However, South Korea shows that a rich country can also reduce the number of female descendants.[115] "Because the dowry is so high, there are 50,000 female fetuses in India which are simply aborted every month. For that reason, the UN has therefore declared the country to be the most dangerous in the world for girls."[116]

There are currently two male births for every female birth in India. Generally, a midwife receives double the fee for a birth when the child is a boy and not a girl. In a country in which the highest state offices have been held by women, there are at the same time millionfold unwanted and unprotected girls.

Gender selection, which takes place millions of times via abortion, is dramatically increasing in those places where boys count significantly more than girls; this is true also, for instance, in the Islamic world, as well as in the Asian countries just mentioned. Indeed, this is because of the overall improving medical care globally. As of 2011, Asia is missing more than 160 million women![117] In India and China, an imbalance has developed within society which is leading to additional attacks on human dignity.

Because of the one-child policy in China (1979-2015), parents had to tremble when it came to their sons. Kidnappings by human traffickers were the order of the day. Their customers were childless couples and parents who had not given birth to the son they desire.[118] We can hope this problem may be in decline since Chinese parents are now allowed to have two children.

There are, however, increasing numbers of gender-related abortions in Europe.[119] In the meantime, this development has been noted even by the

---

[115] "100 Women: How South Korea stopped its parents aborting girls," BBC News, 13 January 2017. https://www.bbc.com/news/world-asia-38362474.

[116] Sophie Mühlmann, „Das Schicksal von Indiens verlorenen Töchtern" (translation of title, "The Fate of India's Lost Daughers"), *Die Welt* (a German newspaper) May 6, 2012. https://www.welt.de/vermischtes/article106264933/Das-Schicksal-von-Indiens-verlorenen-Toechtern.html.

[117] Hasnain Kazim, „Der größte Männerclub der Welt: Abtreibungsfolgen in Asien" (translation of title, "The Largest Boys' Club in the World: The Results of Abortion in Asia"), *Spiegel Online* 6 July 2011. http://www.spiegel.de/panorama/gesellschaft/abtreibungsfolgen-in-asien-der-groesste-maennerclub-der-welt-a-772246.html.

[118] Andrew Jacobs, „In China werden Jungen entführt und verkauft" (translation of title, "In China boys are kidnapped and sold") *Welt* 19 March 2009. https://www.welt.de/politik/article3582329/In-China-werden-Jungen-entfuehrt-und-verkauft.html.

[119] Detlef Drewes and Joachim Bomhard, „Abtreibungen alarmieren Europa" (translation of title: "Abortions are alarming Europe"), *Augsburger Allgemeine* 4 January

German Society for Gynecology and Obstetrics.[120] The Council of Europe stated in a resolution dated November 2011: "Prenatal gender selection has taken on alarming dimensions." In 2009, the national social and health authorities in Sweden realized they could not deny that abortion on the basis of gender was happening. After two daughters, a mother had aborted two additional girls and wanted to abort the third since she wanted to give birth to a boy.

The numbers are particularly alarming in Albania, Armenia, Azerbaijan, and Georgia. The birth rates there indicate that there are 112 newborn boys in comparison to 100 girls.

The International Society for Human Rights has written concerning gendercide in China: "Furthermore, the gender ratio at birth, which as a general rule was around 106 boys per 100 girls, has, since the introduction of the one-child policy, risen to an unnatural and historically unique level. While in the 1953 and 1964 censuses there were still normal gender proportions of 104 boys to 100 girls, by 1982 it had risen to 108. These irregularities continued in the years which followed, and the development even went so far that in 1995 the sex ratio was 116 and then five years later almost 118 per 100 girls. This phenomenon can be traced back to three factors. First, there is low fertility. Second, there is a strong and culturally conditioned preference for sons. And third, there is, in the meantime, widespread availability of prenatal gender determination, which often entails aborting a female fetus. To counter this trend, the Chinese government has started a campaign for more girls in the country. Married couples who decide for the birth of a daughter are rewarded with additional financial retirement benefits and homes. The work of convincing individuals is particularly difficult in rural areas, since it is mostly sons who care for the parents in old age, while daughters marry into the families of their husbands. In the meantime, determining gender prior to birth has been prohibited through the new law. Consequently, doctors are also forbidden, under threat of punishment, from informing parents of the gender of their child."[121]

2013. https://www.augsburger-allgemeine.de/politik/Abtreibungen-alarmieren-Europa-id23373341.html.

[120]   http://www.dggg.de/publikationen/stellungnahmen/?eID=dam_frontend_push &docID=1522, 21.2.2013.

[121]   Christine Pierk, „Das Recht an Kindern hat der Staat: Ein-Kind-Politik in der Volksrepublik China" (translation of title: "The Right to Children Belongs to the State: One-Child Politics in the People's Republic of China"), https://www.igfm.de/china/hintergrund/ein-kind-politik/.

The Risk of Being a Woman

Maternal Mortality

The International Society for Human Rights has written: "Maternal mortality is the death of a woman while pregnant or within 42 days of termination of pregnancy, from any cause related to or aggravated by the pregnancy or its management. Cases of death while pregnant which result from accidental or incidental causes do not count as maternal mortality. The reference value is the number of maternal deaths per 100,000 live births."[122]

"Viewed statistically, there is a woman dying every two minutes somewhere in the world from the consequences of a pregnancy or birth. And yet, the United Nations reports this as positive news since the global average for maternal mortality 20 years ago was twice as high. Therefore, clear progress has been achieved. This is shown in a current article entitled "Trends in Maternal Mortality: 1990 to 2010." According to the report, the numbers of mothers who die annually due to complications during pregnancy or when giving birth dropped from 543,000 to 287,000. This is a decrease of 47%. This is far from sufficient to reach the Millennium Development Goal no. 5, that of reducing the maternal mortality rate. Within individual countries, as well as between countries and regions around the world, there exist great differences. Still, progress has been made in almost every region of the world."[123] Since 1900, maternity mortality has fallen in industrialized countries from about 300 per 100,000 live births to 8-12 per 100,000 because of improved medical care.

Nonetheless, regarding the maternity mortality Millennium Goal of the UN: "Ten countries have even been able to achieve a drop of 75% and thus achieve the Millennium Development Goal: Equatorial Guinea, Belarus, Bhutan, Estonia, Iran, Lithuania, the Maldives, Nepal, Romania, and Vietnam. And yet, in many countries – in particular, in sub-Saharan Africa – the target will not be met by 2015. While the 2010 global average of maternal mortality was 210 deaths per 100,000 live births, the number of deaths in sub-Saharan Africa was 500 women. Of the 40 countries with the highest maternal mortality, 36 are in sub-Saharan Africa. One-third of all cases of death among mothers are attributable to two countries. In 2010, 56,000

---

[122] http://www.bib-demografie.de/SharedDocs/Glossareintraege/DE/M/muetter-sterblichkeit.html.

[123] http://www.menschliche-entwicklung-staerken.de/news00.html?&no_cache=1 &tx_ttnews%5Btt_news%5D=1068&cHash=b7843fcdf309034bcc3dbe068d8480c3.

mothers died in India and 40,000 in Nigeria. That amounted to 20 percent and 14 percent of all deaths, respectively."[124]

HIV/AIDS

Around the world, there are 30 million people living with HIV, half of whom are women. In sub-Saharan Africa, where the pandemic has spread most strongly, women increasingly comprise the majority of those infected.[125] In those parts of Africa where studies are available, but also in the Caribbean, young women between the ages of 15 and 24 become infected with HIV six times more frequently than do men of the same age.

The guilt lies with massive numbers of rapes in areas where there have been wars, often civil wars, as well as domestic violence, and with the lack of female self-determination over their bodies and their behavior. Women often have less information about sexually transmitted diseases, hardly have access to contraceptives, and often are not able to decide for themselves whether contraceptives are used as protection against HIV. Marriage also does not provide protection against HIV if the male partner has become infected somewhere else and refuses to take protective measures. Once it has become known that women are HIV positive, they are often discriminated against more strongly than are men. Even in the Western world, it is infected men – and not only those who are homosexual – who are more firmly placed in the center of attention at AIDS galas and campaigns than are women. Additionally, it is often taken for granted that women care for those family members infected with HIV or, for example, AIDS orphans.

A study published in 2004 covering 1,366 women in South Africa, whom health centers searched out for HIV tests, showed that a one and one-half times greater percentage of women are HIV positive if they are beaten and dominated by their husbands or are completely dependent upon their partner than if they are in nonviolent relationships.[126]

---

[124] Ibid.

[125] http://www.unifem.org/gender_issues/hiv_aids/index.html;   http://www.genderandaids.org/.

[126] Kristin L Dunkle and others, "Gender-based violence, relationship power, and risk of HIV infection in women attending antenatal clinics in South Africa," The Lancet: 363(9419) 2004, p. 1415.

Exclusion from Education

Even if great progress has been made in recent decades and women and girls are learning to read and write, two-thirds of all illiterate people around the world are female.[127] Girls make up 56 percent of the 77 million children who never go to school. Even accounting for large regional differences, such as some areas where women are more well educated than men, if looked at globally, women suffer discrimination in regard to education.

In large parts of the world, girls less frequently go to school. As students, they miss school more often because of tasks they must fulfill at home, they go to school for a shorter period of time, and they seldom go on to upper level schools. When parents or families are faced with the choice of whether the son or the daughter should be enabled to receive the better education, in many countries it is still boys who are favored. A reversal in the relationship has been noted in some Western countries. For instance, it is predominantly women who are school teachers in the West. Girls now have greater opportunities in school, receive better grades, and are more popular with teachers. Indeed, in the USA there are many more women who receive college degrees than men.[128] Still, when looked at on a global scale, the discrimination seen in earlier times persists. In some countries, girls do not go to school because they must help their mother at home with younger siblings or because they must work in the fields. They might have the task of fetching water very early from a well (which might be some hours away) and simply do not have time left for school.

In some Muslim-majority countries, it is not considered proper for girls to go alone to school or to be taught by a male instructor in school. Therefore, they stay home. In some schools – for instance, in Yemen – there are no toilets for girls. Such circumstances can also prevent girls from attending school.

In Iran at the time of the Shah and to the present, there are more women students than men. At present approximately 60 percent of all individuals commencing studies are women, but women have been prohibited from pursuing 70 courses of study.[129]

At our latitude, education for women in the Middle Ages was largely limited to convents, to which mostly only girls from wealthy families had access. Beginning in the sixteenth century, women's orders were established. They developed places of education for women to teach them to

---

[127] Seager, *Atlas*, 78-79.
[128] Seager, *Atlas*, 80-83.
[129] https://en.wikipedia.org/wiki/Women%27s_education_in_Iran.

read and write as well as to convey handicraft and homemaking skills. It was not until the beginning of the women's movement in the final quarter of the nineteenth century that higher education for women became a topic. Associations for women's education were established which especially addressed the typical arguments that women could not, did not want to, or should not obtain higher education.

Poverty

When hunger rules, women are more affected by it. When medical care is lacking, women are more affected by it. Estimates are that 70 percent of the poor are female, but unfortunately no comprehensive global study on this topic exists. Poor women have a more difficult time borrowing money than do poor men. In most countries in Africa, the Near East, and South Asia, inheritance law and practice prevent women from having significant property or other possessions.[130] At the same time, poor women are less protected against violence, exploitation, a lack of rights, and dishonesty than are poor men.

In many countries and cultures there is much manual work which is largely left to women, such as fetching water, agriculture, and the production of food. Even in those places where women carry the major burden of work and of sustaining life, they may have to also run the household and care for the children.

According to a UNICEF study dating from 2007, 70 percent of the agricultural work is conducted by women, and 90 percent of foodstuffs in several regions of the world are generated by women.[131] An investigation in Mexico in 2006 looked at how much men and women worked inside the home when both were equally occupied with other jobs. In such cases, women performed 33 additional hours of work per week in the home, and men performed six additional hours of work.[132] In South Africa there are areas without running water where women are responsible for carrying water in containers. UN Women found in 2007 that all women taken together walked the distance to the moon (394,400 kilometers) and back 16 times per day.[133]

Significant drivers of human trafficking, particularly of women, are poverty, the lack of education, and the absence of protection for women.

---

[130]   See Seager, *Atlas*, 86-91.
[131]   UNICEF, *Women and Children: The Double Dividend of Gender Equality*, 2007.
[132]   UNDP, *Water and Human Development Report*, 2006.
[133]   UNIFEM, "Progress of Arab Women," *Jordanian News Digest*, 26 February 2007.

At this point prevention should set in.[134] Combating poverty is an important preventive measure in the fight against human trafficking. Women affected come largely from countries which are economically weak or find themselves in the midst of political change. Women are frequently most affected by unemployment, low wages, violence, and economic hardship. Because of a general lack of prospects, women get into a situation in which they can be exploited by human traffickers. A family which cannot feed its children may give away its daughters (and sometimes the sons as well) in hopes that the labor broker can procure them a good job as household help or in a company. A single mother who cannot provide for her children in her home country is prepared to try her fortune elsewhere. Human traffickers often exploit these situations. Women and children then become the victims of human traffickers who treat them as merchandise and place them in cacao plantations in the Ivory Coast or in the commercial sex industry in Germany.[135]

Dispossession of Rights

In predominantly Islamic countries, women are only granted limited rights within the family – above all, in rural areas or where poverty and a lack of education rule. Even among the upper classes, the right to file for divorce is possible in only a few narrowly defined cases. For instance, one situation is where financial support is not being paid by the husband. The wife must strive to receive even a court proceeding, while for the husband, divorce is significantly easier. This is the case even where Islamic majority countries have limited the opportunities husbands traditionally have had to break with their wives.

Generally, women are also disadvantaged when it comes to the question of the custody of children. According to Sharia law, in cases of divorce, the husband has a claim on children who are past infancy. This means that after a divorce and beginning at an age of about 7 to 14 for girls and 3 to 7 for boys, the children are part of the family of the husband, and under certain circumstances the mother never sees the children again.

---

[134] Kurt Bangert, *Kinderarmut in Deutschland und weltweit* (translation of title: *Childhood Poverty in Germany and Worldwide*," Holzgerlingen: SCM Hänssler, 2010); Andreas Kusch and Thomas Schirrmacher (eds.), *Der Kampf gegen die weltweite Armut* (Bonn: VKW, 2009); Kurt Bangert and Thomas Schirrmacher (eds.), *HIV und AIDS als christliche Herausforderung* (Bonn: VKW, 2008).

[135] http://frauenwerk.org/netzwerk/pages/was-kann-ich-tun/armut-bekaempfen.php, no date provided.

It is not always Sharia law that can be blamed for the discrimination against women and their being dispossessed of most of their rights. Common law and tradition are frequently even more restrictive. Alternatively, tribal law can maintain far more sustained discrimination, as is the case in Afghanistan. For instance, tribal law allows an exchange of wives to settle a conflict, and tribal law allows bequeathing a widow to a brother of the deceased individual without the wife having a right to a say in the matter. Additionally, girls are denied attending school more out of concern for tradition or for the reputation of the family than because of Sharia law, which endorses the acquisition of education by both genders. Tribal law in Libya and Yemen is also more misogynistic than Sharia law.

Excluded from Suffrage

New Zealand was the first country in the world to give women the right to vote.[136] Australia followed in 1902 and allowed women to run for office. However, Australia excluded "colored" individuals and Aborigines until 1962. In 1906, Finland, at the time an 'independent grand duchy of Russia,' became the first government in Europe to give women the right to vote. In 1917, Azerbaijan became the first Islamic country to introduce women's suffrage. Russia followed in 1917, with Germany, Austria, and Great Britain following in 1918. Until 1929, Great Britain only extended voting rights to women over the age of 30. In the USA, the territory of Wyoming, which officially became a state in 1890, began to offer women the right to vote in 1869. The right to vote was extended to women at the federal level in 1920, after the first woman had been voted into Congress in 1916. However, it was not until 1965 that African-American women were given the right to vote.

The way to women's suffrage in some countries has been rocky. The Senate of France rejected women's voting rights, and it was only through a 1944 order that they were able to be introduced. In Portugal and Spain, it was not until the end of their respective dictatorships in the 1970s that women's suffrage was able to be introduced.

Women's right to vote failed in two referenda in Lichtenstein in 1971 and 1973 and only came about in 1984. Switzerland experienced difficulties in several cantons, although the Swiss Supreme Court forced the final canton, Canton Appenzell-Innerrhoden, to expand the designation of "Swiss citizen" in its constitution. The reason for the problems in Switzerland and Lichtenstein was a process of referenda with predominately male voters.

---

[136]   See the chart in Seager, *Atlas*, 94-95.

If that had been the case in other countries, the right for women to vote would have surely also been long delayed elsewhere.

In Latin America, most countries moved to women's suffrage in the 1930s, while in Asia it has occurred gradually over a long period of time, from Mongolia in 1920 up to the present day, to Syria and Lebanon in 1953, the first Arab countries to offer women the right to vote. Women voted for the first time in Kuwait in 2007, and there are a number of Arab countries still missing from the list.

At the same time, there have repeatedly been peculiarities. In Belgium, Italy, and Bulgaria, only married women were initially allowed to vote. The question of whether the right to vote was to be withdrawn from unmarried men never came up. In Scandinavia and Great Britain, the opposite was the case. Only single and widowed ladies were allowed to vote in local elections since wives were already represented by their husbands. In Greece, a minimum education level was initially introduced for women – not for men – when it came to the right to vote.

There is still no right to vote for women in Brunei. In Saudi Arabia, as promised in 2011, women received the vote in 2015. Of course, women do not vote in countries without elections, such as the Vatican and the United Arab Emirates. In Bhutan, every family has a vote. Furthermore, women in Lebanon – and not men – must demonstrate they have received a school education when they go to vote.

The arguments against granting women's suffrage have been strikingly similar in all cultures, namely that women have no interest in politics, that because of a lack of education or other higher priority interest in housekeeping, they are not in a position to vote, that they are not in a position to judge political issues and instead vote purely emotionally – as if only men are all political professionals and free of emotions. Finally, there is the argument that a danger would exist that women would then have further demands about holding office and exerting influence.

By the way, women vote strikingly differently than do men in all countries around the world without there being a strict, globally valid explanation for the differences regarding strong or weak preferences with respect to certain individuals, parties, programs, or issues.

Little Chance of Becoming a Head of State

Between 1960 and 1979, there were four women who became the first female heads of state around the world. In 1960, Sirimawo Bandaranaike (1916–2000) became the first female head of government by becoming the Prime Minister of Ceylon, which is today called Sri Lanka. Indira Gandhi

(1917–1984) became Prime Minister of India in 1966; Golda Meir (1898–1978) won Prime Minister of Israel in 1969; and Margaret Thatcher (1925–2013) became the first female Prime Minister of Great Britain in 1979.

The first democratically elected female head of state was Vigdís Finnbogadóttir (b. 1930). She was the President of Iceland from 1980 to 1996. Before that, there were female prime ministers who were installed on an interim basis or who took over the office from their husbands as widows, such as Martínez de Perón (b. 1931), from 1974–1976 in Argentina. What followed were several small states, such as Iceland, with female prime ministers. The first large country with a female president was the Philippines with Corazón Aquino (1933–2009), who was the widow of the previous president.

Women are not only victims.

In conclusion, we would like to make clear what we *do not* want to say. We do not want to convey the idea that women are always the victim and never the offender or that women are not able to try to justify, advocate, or exercise violence. Women are not automatically "better people." The British Prime Minister Margaret Thatcher conducted the Falklands War. The radical feminist Andrea Dworkin proceeds on the assumption that every man exudes "terror" and allowed herself the following gaffe: "I want to see a man beaten to a bloody pulp ..."[137] – tragic given her overall accomplishments. During the civil war in Rwanda, the female Rwandan Minister for Family and the Promotion of Women called upon the Hutu militia to rape Tutsi women and girls.[138]

Contrary to the case of the drug cartels, human trafficking is not merely the domain of men. Women represent the largest group of victims; they also occupy an important role as culprits.[139] The United Nations Office on Drugs and Crime (UNODC) wrote in 2009: "Within the framework of an analysis of the offender's profile, it was first determined that women also play an important role as an active party in international human trafficking. This was revealed in criminal statistics in 46 of the 155 countries studied which authorized an analysis according to age, gender, and nationality of human traffickers. In 14 of the 46 countries, there were more women

---

[137]   Andrea Dworkin, *Pornographie* (Frankfurt: Fischer, 1997), 93-94.
[138]   *New York Times*, September 15, 2002.
[139]   „Vereinte Nationen: ‚Menschenhandel nimmt zu,‘" *Newsletter Migration und Bevölkerung* 3/2009.

than men who were prosecuted for human trafficking."[140] "In Eastern Europe and Central Asia, they even represent over 60% of all convicted offenders. 'In these areas it is the norm that women traffic women,' stated Antonio Maria Costa, Executive Director of the United Nations Office on Drugs and Crime (UNODC)."[141]

Violence against women has often become so much a part of culture and society that women themselves not only put up with it but make talking about it taboo. Rather, from a young age, the women suffering such violence internalize it, consider it normal, and even justify it and defend the offenders. They believe that they deserve nothing more: In India, about 70 percent of women find it acceptable for a husband to hit them if they burn a meal, deny sex, or go out without asking him beforehand.

The domestic, family, or social taboo status and trivialization of violence against women is one of the greatest hindrances in the battle against this violence. Women, like men, are just as involved in the taboo status and the trivialization – just as there are women and men who fight against it.

A good example for making it taboo is the fact that mothers often overlook clear signs that their daughter is being sexually abused by relatives or spouses or even vehemently defend the involved men when others voice their suspicion. Even when they are hit, they often play down the offense and declare that it seldom happens, that they have reconciled, and that the husband is otherwise not like that at all. Often, they must first be in counseling, in a women's shelter, or under pastoral care to have their eyes opened.

The horrible fact of female genital mutilation ("female circumcision" discussed above) is less forced by men than by women in the affected cultures. Women employ this procedure on their daughters and commit this torment against them, although they have experienced on their own bodies the torment involved in every case of circumcision. Experience demonstrates that above all, good education and enlightenment can overcome this internalization of violence against women.

Women, and not only men, are violent toward their partners and families. Thus, there is a research discussion as to whether domestic violence is truly only a male issue or whether the consequences of domestic violence only more severely affect women because men are physically

---

[140] Ibid.

[141] Merle Schmalenbach, „Frauen mischen im Menschenhandel mit" (translation of title: "Women are participating in human trafficking"), *Spiegel online* 13 Febraty 2009. http://www.spiegel.de/politik/ausland/uno-bericht-frauen-mischen-im-menschenhandel-mit-a-607364.html.

stronger most of the time. That is very difficult to answer since studies of violence almost exclusively refer to women as victims. This is a scientific and moral one-sidedness which surely cannot be justified. The German Ministry for the Family never moved beyond a small 2005 pilot study, *Violence against Men*, which yielded shocking results.[142] A likewise alarming study by the Evangelical Church in Germany's efforts on issues regarding the male gender was not initially published.[143]

One must always differentiate. Overall, there are more men murdered than women.[144] However, women are significantly more frequently murdered by their partners, relatives, and friends. The life expectancy of women is higher than that of men in practically all countries around the world. Despite that, access to healthcare in many of the poorer countries is much more difficult for women than for men. In the case of honor killings, men appear to be victims as frequently as women. Where stoning is law and is practiced, men are occasionally affected, even if it is the case that women are more frequently affected.

In the meantime, in Western countries, we are now seeing that women have so outperformed men that special programs are being discussed for boys and men. Whoever wants to address the problem that boys always do more poorly in German schools than do girls or that men are always more difficult to motivate for preventive health care should not lose sight of the fact that women are discriminated against.[145] Only ideologues play forms of discrimination off against each other.

---

[142] *Gewalt gegen Männer: Personale Gewaltwiderfahrnisse von Männern in Deutschland* (translation of title: *Violence against Men: Personal Experiences of Violence of Men in Germany*) (Berlin: Bundesministerium für Familie, 2005). https://www.bmfsfj.de/bmfsfj/studie--gewalt-gegen-maenner/84660.

[143] Miriam Hollstein and Freia Peters, „Männer häufiger Opfer von Gewalt als Frauen: Beide Geschlechter sind fast gleich oft Täter – aber Männer schlagen häufiger, Frauen wählen subtilere Mittel" (translation of title: "Men are more frequently the victims of violence than women: the genders are offenders equally as often; men more frequently use their fists while women use more subtle means"), *Die Welt* 12 November 2010. https://www.welt.de/print/die_welt/politik/article 10884320/Neue-Studie-Maenner-haeufiger-Opfer-von-Gewalt-als-Frauen.html. Because of the numbers in this study, one should also see Peter Döge, *Männer – die ewigen Gewalttäter?* (Wiesbaden: Verlag für Sozialwissenschaften, 2013, 2nd Edition).

[144] See Seager, *Atlas*, 30-31.

[145] The discussion is depicted in a balanced fashion in Thomas Gesterkamp, „Für Männer, aber nicht für Frauen," *Aus Politik und Zeitgeschichte* (Themenheft *Mannsbilder*) 62 (2012) 40: pp. 3-10.

By the same token, there are also many types of violence and discrimination where studies have demonstrated in detail that the bulk of offenders are men and the bulk of victims are women. That there are also spheres in which men and women are equally affected should not serve as justification for relativizing the many more frequent spheres and issues where this is not the case.

Domestic violence between partners not only occurs in the case of heterosexual pairs. It also occurs in same-sex pairs of both genders. In such cases, a dominant partner can also exercise power through violence, including sexualized violence.[146]

In this book, though we have mentioned counter-examples, these generalizations should be remembered: Ninety-nine percent of all offenders in the case of rape are male, and 80 percent of the victims are female; 80 percent of all people affected by human trafficking are women, since the sexual exploitation of women is more widespread.

---

[146] See Holger Walther, „Häusliche Gewalt in gleichgeschlechtlichen Partnerschaften" (translation of title: "Domestic Violence in Same-sex Partnerships"), VLSP, 2016. https://www.vlsp.de/wissenschaft/partnerschaft/gewalt.

Appendix: Our Christian Motivation

Efforts against violence towards women and against oppression and discrimination against women should bring all people of good will together, regardless of religion or worldview. Despite this, we want to briefly sketch our motivation for this book. This is not the place to justify this in any detailed manner or to grapple with the history of Christianity or other notions.

According to the creation account, God created men and women according to his own image and with equal dignity: "So God created man in his own image, in the image of God he created him, male and female he created them" (Genesis 1:27). The requirement upon people to love God and neighbor arises from this human dignity. As a pattern of love, the relationship between husband and wife is the place in which children are brought into the world, are loved, and are raised to the point of independence.

Love as a fundamental principle, affected by sin and evil on the part of people, goes in completely the opposite direction of hate, violence, the exercise of power, and egoism. Unfortunately, these issues find their expression where people spend the most time, namely in marriages, partnerships, and families, as well as in work relationships. Evil can corrupt a relationship, for instance, when a father, whose role is supposed to mean love, warmth, protection, and encouragement for children to become independent, instead, through abuse, does just the opposite to children. Jesus' death on the cross and resurrection from the dead accomplished forgiveness of sin and reconciliation with God and made peace between men and women and between parents and children possible. This peace is also specifically available for relationships between the sexes. At the same time, forgiveness does not mean to make a taboo of, or to trivialize, what happens between people. Rather, it presupposes an unsparing disclosure and acknowledgement of guilt.

Human dignity not only leads to love as the best way of dealing with each other. It also justifies equal human rights for all people, namely, that which is each person's due, which is indeed necessary to live as human beings. Wherever human rights are violated, God has commissioned the state to restore peace and justice, to restrain evil, and, when it has occurred, to mete out punishment (Romans 13:1-7).

Sexuality in biblical thought is never set in relation to one's own person. Rather, it is always set in relation to one's partner. Thus, love's expression is not to desire to have power and exercise force over the other, to have the best for oneself. Rather, the central thought is that my needs and self are not to be in the foreground. Instead, it is the needs of the other person that should come first. I understand by this that, in the final event, it also serves me when I invest in other people. Whoever marries must serve the other (1 Corinthians 7:32-34) – and that applies to both genders. Paul writes in 1 Corinthians 7:3, 4 that the secret of sexuality is that the woman does not belong to herself but to her husband. Also, the husband does not belong to himself but to the wife. This sexual equality and the notion of thinking about the other places all of a husband's longings for power into question: "The man should fulfil his marital duty to his wife, and likewise the wife to her husband . . . In the same way, the husband's body does not belong to him alone but also to his wife."

Accordingly, we do not believe that abolishing the family would also abolish discrimination against women. Experience also speaks against this. Instead, marriage and family, precisely by being aware of the dangers, can become a place where protection against violence as well as observance of tolerance are able to be practiced extensively.[147] We need "modern fathers" more than ever.[148]

In addition to equality on the basis of common human dignity, there is a second motivation for us as Christians: The call to help those in distress and to be an advocate for those who are too weak, or addicted, in order that they might help themselves. This concept plays a central role in the Bible. We read in Proverbs 31:8, 9: "Speak up for those who cannot speak for themselves, for the rights of all who are destitute. Speak up and judge fairly, defend the rights of the poor and needy."

By way of example, this is brought to bear in the call to tackle the exploitation of widows and orphans. This is found 100 times in the Bible. Job 22:8, 9 criticizes aptly: ". . . though you were a powerful man, owning land – an honored man, living on it . . . you sent widows away empty and broke the strength of the fatherless." And Jesus makes the following denouncement: "They devour widows' houses and for a show make lengthy prayers. Such men will be punished most severely" (Mark 12:40). In contrast, the call goes out in Exodus 22:22: "Do not take advantage of a widow or an orphan," and in Deuteronomy 10:18: "He [God] defends the cause of the fatherless and the widow, and loves the alien, giving him food and clothing."

---

[147] See Thomas Schirrmacher, *Der Segen von Ehe und Familie* (Bonn: VKW, 2006) and Thomas Schirrmacher, *Moderne Väter: Weder Waschlappen noch Despot* (SCM Hänssler, 2007).

[148] This is part of the title of a forthcoming book by Thomas Schirrmacher, *Modern Fathers.*

Likewise, in Isaiah 1:17 one reads: ". . . learn to do right! Seek justice, encourage the oppressed. Defend the cause of the fatherless, plead the case of the widow."

Even if "widows" have a lot to do with the issue of women's rights, we assume that we are not too literally limit ourselves to "widows" and "orphans," especially as there are indeed "widows and orphans" who are doing well and who are provided for. Instead, it has more to do with all of those who are oppressed by the powerful and who cannot help themselves. Regardless of the situation and which human rights issue is at stake, we have a duty to those in need – the hungry, those suffering from AIDS, those who are not cared for, those forced into prostitution, people who because of corruption are deprived of their rights, street children, and abused children.

Bibliography

Websites

For more information about violence against women, one can read many good websites. Some places to start:

Terres des Femmes is a German women's rights organization that works internationally in English. Their slogan is "Women's rights are human rights! We are engaged to promote a just world in which women and girls have the rights to self-determination, freedom, and to live with dignity." Website: https://www.frauenrechte.de/online/en/.

The Council of Europe's Gender Equality Commission provides much helpful information, especially about domestic violence and violence against women. Website: https://www.coe.int/en/web/gender equality.

The European Union has extensive programming to support women's rights and to overcome violence against women. Website: https://ec.europa.eu/europeaid/sectors/human-rights-and-gover nance/democracy-and-human-rights/anti-discrimination-moveme nts/women_en.

UN Women, more formally the UN Commission on the Status of Women, has been a global center for the just treatment of women since 1947. Website: http://www.unwomen.org/en.

The World Health Organization, department of Women's Health, provides information regarding the medical dimensions of violence against women, as well as other medical needs of women. Website: https://www.who.int/topics/womens_health/en/.

The US Center for Disease Control and Prevention (CDC) has a women's health initiative aimed at equity between men and women in health care. The CDC also publishes reports on violence against women. Website: https://www.cdc.gov/women/index.htm.

The US Department of Justice has an Office on Violence Against Women. Though oriented toward problems in the US, some of their information is of interest internationally. Some of the website is in Spanish. Website: https://www.justice.gov/ovw.

The Gendercide Awareness Project brings attention to the many millions of women and girls who die by neglect or intent. Website: https://www.gendap.org/index.html.

The Global Center for Women and Justice is a research and educational initiative based in a Christian university dedicated to justice for women. Website: https://www.vanguard.edu/research/gcwj.

UN Reports, International Reports, Statistics

http://www.unwomen.org/

http://www.unifem.org/gender_issues/violence_against_women/facts_figures.html

http://en.wikipedia.org/wiki/Global_Gender_Gap_Report

UN women. Progress of the World's Women 2011-2012. 2011, http://progress.unwomen.org/pdfs/EN-Report-Progress.pdf

Global Gender Gap Report 2012, http://www.weforum.org/issues/global-gender-gap

Global and regional estimates of violence against women: prevalence and health effects of intimate partner violence and non-partner sexual violence. World Health Organization: Geneva, 2013, https://www.who.int/reproductivehealth/publications/violence/9789241564625/en/index.html

UN Women – Violence Against Women Prevalence Data: Surveys By Country (2011). http://www.womenlobby.org/spip.php?article2169&lang=en

http://www.unifem.org/gender_issues/violence_against_women/facts_figures.html

World Bank Group. World Development Report 2012: Gender Equality and Development. http://siteresources.worldbank.org/INTWDR2012/Resources/7778105-1299699968583/7786210-1315936222006/Complete-Report.pdf

OECD. Atlas of Gender and Development: How Social Norms Affect Gender Equality in non-OECD Countries. 2010, http://www.oecd.org/berlin/publikationen/atlasofgenderanddevelopment.htm

Joni Seager. The Penguin Atlas of Women in the World: Fourth Edition. London: Penguin, 2008 (zuletzt übersetzt wurde die Ausgabe von 1998: Der Fischer Frauen-Atlas)

Violence against Women generally

www.frauenrechte.de/en/ (Terre fes femmes)

http://www.gendercide.org/case.html

http://en.wikipedia.org/wiki/Gendercide

Sheila Jeffreys: The Industrial Vagina. The Political Economy of the Global Sex Trade. London / New York: Routledge, 2009

Diana E. H. Russell, Roberta A. Ahrmes (ed.). *Femicide in Global Perspective.* Teachers College Press: New York, 2001

Domestic Violence

Shannan M. Catalano, *Intimate Partner Violence, 1993-2010*, Bureau of Justice Statistics, 27.12.2012, http://www.bjs.gov/index.cfm?ty=pbdetail &iid=4536

War

http://www.unifem.org/gender_issues/women_war_peace/conflict_rela ted_sexual_violence.html

Forced Marriage and Rape

https://en.wikipedia.org/wiki/Forced_marriage

https://en.wikipedia.org/wiki/Child_marriage

https://en.wikipedia.org/wiki/Rape

Gendercide through Abortion

www.gendercide.org

Jugal Kishore. *The Female Feticide.* Saarbrücken: Lambert, 2012

Darshan Kaur Narang, Neelam Kavita Koradia. *Female Feticide and Infanticide.* Saarbrücken: Lambert, 2013

Maternal Mortality

Trends in maternal mortality: 1990 to 2010, http://www.unfpa.org/web dav/site/global/shared/documents/publications/2012/Trends_in_ maternal_mortality_A4-1.pdf

Genital Mutilation/Female Circumcision

http://www.who.int/mediacentre/factsheets/fs241/en/

Female Trafficking

Combating Trafficking as Modern-Day Slavery. 2010 Annual Report of the Special Representative and Co-ordinator for Combating Trafficking in Human Beings. Wien: OSCE, 2010, www.osce.org/cthb/74730

US Department of State: *Trafficking in Persons Report 2010*. Washington, 2010, http://www.state.gov/g/tip/rls/tiprpt/2010/ (Berichte zu allen Ländern)

Thomas Schirrmacher. Human Trafficking. WEA Global Issues Series. VKW: Bonn, 2015, Download: https://www.iirf.eu/journal-books/global-issues-series/human-trafficking/

Pornography

(in German, Romanian and Russian) Thomas Schirrmacher. *Internetpornografie*. Holzgerlingen: SCM Hänssler, 2008

Diana E. H. Russell. "Femicidal Pornography," pp. 50-60 in: Diana E. H. Russell, Roberta A. Ahrmes (eds.). *Femicide in Global Perspective*. Teachers College Press: New York, 2001

Honor Killings

https://en.wikipedia.org/wiki/Honor_killing

(in German) Christine Schirrmacher. Mord im Namen der ‚Ehre' zwischen Migration und Tradition. Rechtspolitisches Forum – Legal Policy Forum 37. Trier: Institut für Rechtspolitik an der Universität Trier, 2007

HIV/AIDS

http://www.unifem.org/gender_issues/hiv_aids/index.html

http://www.genderandaids.org/

(in German) Kurt Bangert, Thomas Schirrmacher (eds.). *HIV und AIDS als christliche Herausforderung*. 2 Vols. VKW: Bonn, 2008

Educational Disadvantages; Poverty

http://en.wikipedia.org/wiki/Sex_differences_in_education

http://www.unifem.org/gender_issues/women_poverty_economics/index.html

UNESCO. *World Atlas of Gender Equality in Education.* http://www.unesco.org/new/en/education/themes/leading-the-international-agenda/gender-and-education/resources/the-world-atlas-of-gender-equality-in-education/

UNESCO. *Global Education Monitoring Report 2019.* https://en.unesco.org/gem-report/taxonomy/term/210

Islam und Scharia

Christine Schirrmacher. The Sharia. WEA Global Issues Series. VKW: Bonn, 2013. Download: https://www.iirf.eu/journal-books/global-issues-series/the-sharia-law-and-order-in-islam/

Christine Schirrmacher. Islam and Society. WEA Global Issues Series. VKW: Bonn, 2008. Download: https://www.iirf.eu/journal-books/global-issues-series/islam-and-society/

Christine Schirrmacher, Ursula Spuler-Stegemann. *Frauen und die Scharia - Die Menschenrechte im Islam.* München: Diedrichs 2004; Bergisch-Gladbach: BasteiLübbe, 2006

P. Newton; M. Rafiqul Haqq. *The Place of Women in Pure Islam.* Pioneer Book Company: Caney, 1994[3]

World Evangelical Alliance

World Evangelical Alliance is a global ministry working with local churches around the world to join in common concern to live and proclaim the Good News of Jesus in their communities. WEA is a network of churches in 129 nations that have each formed an evangelical alliance and over 100 international organizations joining together to give a worldwide identity, voice and platform to more than 600 million evangelical Christians. Seeking holiness, justice and renewal at every level of society – individual, family, community and culture, God is glorified and the nations of the earth are forever transformed.

Christians from ten countries met in London in 1846 for the purpose of launching, in their own words, "a new thing in church history, a definite organization for the expression of unity amongst Christian individuals belonging to different churches." This was the beginning of a vision that was fulfilled in 1951 when believers from 21 countries officially formed the World Evangelical Fellowship. Today, 150 years after the London gathering, WEA is a dynamic global structure for unity and action that embraces 600 million evangelicals in 129 countries. It is a unity based on the historic Christian faith expressed in the evangelical tradition. And it looks to the future with vision to accomplish God's purposes in discipling the nations for Jesus Christ.

Commissions:

- Theology
- Missions
- Religious Liberty
- Women's Concerns
- Youth
- Information Technology

Initiatives and Activities

- Ambassador for Human Rights
- Ambassador for Refugees
- Creation Care Task Force
- Global Generosity Network
- International Institute for Religious Freedom
- International Institute for Islamic Studies
- Leadership Institute
- Micah Challenge
- Global Human Trafficking Task Force
- Peace and Reconciliation Initiative
- UN-Team

Church Street Station
P.O. Box 3402
New York, NY 10008-3402
Phone +[1] 212 233 3046
Fax +[1] 646-957-9218
www.worldea.org

WEA
World Evangelical Alliance

Giving Hands

GIVING HANDS GERMANY (GH) was established in 1995 and is officially recognized as a nonprofit foreign aid organization. It is an international operating charity that – up to now – has been supporting projects in about 40 countries on four continents. In particular we care for orphans and street children. Our major focus is on Africa and Central America. GIVING HANDS always mainly provides assistance for self-help and furthers human rights thinking.

The charity itself is not bound to any church, but on the spot we are co-operating with churches of all denominations. Naturally we also cooperate with other charities as well as governmental organizations to provide assistance as effective as possible under the given circumstances.

The work of GIVING HANDS GERMANY is controlled by a supervisory board. Members of this board are Manfred Feldmann, Colonel V. Doner and Kathleen McCall. Dr. Christine Schirrmacher is registered as legal manager of GIVING HANDS at the local district court. The local office and work of the charity are coordinated by Rev. Horst J. Kreie as executive manager. Dr. theol. Thomas Schirrmacher serves as a special consultant for all projects.

Thanks to our international contacts companies and organizations from many countries time and again provide containers with gifts in kind which we send to the different destinations where these goods help to satisfy elementary needs. This statutory purpose is put into practice by granting nutrition, clothing, education, construction and maintenance of training centers at home and abroad, construction of wells and operation of water treatment systems, guidance for self-help and transportation of goods and gifts to areas and countries where needy people live.

GIVING HANDS has a publishing arm under the leadership of Titus Vogt, that publishes human rights and other books in English, Spanish, Swahili and other languages.

These aims are aspired to the glory of the Lord according to the basic Christian principles put down in the Holy Bible.

Baumschulallee 3a • D-53115 Bonn • Germany
Phone: +49 / 228 / 695531 • Fax +49 / 228 / 695532
www.gebende-haende.de • info@gebende-haende.de

International Institute for Religious Freedom

Purpose and Aim

The "International Institute for Religious Freedom" (IIRF) is a network of professors, researchers, academics, specialists and university institutions from all continents with the aim of working towards:

- The establishment of reliable facts on the restriction of religious freedom worldwide.

- The making available of results of such research to other researchers, politicians, advocates, as well as the media.

- The introduction of the subject of religious freedom into academic research and curricula.

- The backing up of advocacy for victims of violations of religious freedom in the religious, legal and political world.

- Serving discriminated and persecuted believers and academics wherever they are located. Publications and other research will be made available as economically and as readily available as possible to be affordable in the Global South.

Tools

The IIRF encourages all activities that contribute to the understanding of religious freedom. These include:

- Dissemination of existing literature, information about archives, compilation of bibliographies etc.

- Production and dissemination of new papers, journals and books.

- Gathering and analysis of statistics and evidence.

- Supplying of ideas and materials to universities and institutions of theological education to encourage the inclusion of religious freedom issues into curricula.

- Guiding postgraduate students in research projects either personally or in cooperation with the universities and educational institutions.

- Representation at key events where opportunity is given to strengthen connections with the wider religious liberty community and with politicians, diplomats and media.

Online / Contact:

- www.iirf.eu / info@iirf.eu

Institute of Islamic Studies

The protestant "Institute of Islamic Studies" is a network of scholars in Islamic studies and is carried out by the Evangelical Alliance in Germany, Austria and Switzerland.

Churches, the political arena, and society at large are provided foundational information relating to the topic of 'Islam' through research and the presentation thereof via publications, adult education seminars, and democratic political discourse.

Research Focus

As far as our work is concerned, the focus is primarily on Islam in Europe, the global development of Islamic theology and of Islamic fundamentalism, as well as a respectful and issue-related meeting of Christians and Muslims. In the process, misunderstandings about Islam and Muslims can be cleared up, and problematic developments in Islamic fundamentalism and political Islam are explained. Through our work we want to contribute to engaging Muslims in an informed and fair manner.

What we do

Lectures, seminars, and conferences for public authorities, churches, political audiences, and society at large

- Participation in special conferences on the topic of Islam
- The publication of books in German, English, and Spanish
- The preparation of scholarly studies for the general public
- Special publications on current topics
- Production of a German-English journal entitled "Islam and Christianity"
- Regular press releases with commentaries on current events from a scholarly Islamic studies perspective
- Academic surveys and experts' reports for advisory boards of government
- Regular news provided as summaries of Turkish and Arab language internet publications
- Fatwa archive
- Website with a collection of articles

Martin Bucer Seminary

Faithful to biblical truth
Cooperating with the Evangelical Alliance
Reformed

Solid training for the Kingdom of God

- Alternative theological education
- Study while serving a church or working another job
- Enables students to remain in their own churches
- Encourages independent thinking
- Learning from the growth of the universal church.

Academic

- For the Bachelor's degree: 180 Bologna-Credits
- For the Master's degree: 120 additional Credits
- Both old and new teaching methods: All day seminars, independent study, term papers, etc.

Our Orientation:

- Complete trust in the reliability of the Bible
- Building on reformation theology
- Based on the confession of the German Evangelical Alliance
- Open for innovations in the Kingdom of God

Our Emphasis:

- The Bible
- Ethics and Basic Theology
- Missions
- The Church

Our Style:

- Innovative
- Relevant to society
- International
- Research oriented
- Interdisciplinary

Structure

- 15 study centers in 7 countries with local partners
- 5 research institutes
- President: Prof. Dr. Thomas Schirrmacher
  Vice President: Prof. Dr. Thomas K. Johnson
- Deans: Thomas Kinker, Th.D.;
  Titus Vogt, lic. theol., Carsten Friedrich, M.Th.

Missions through research

- Institute for Religious Freedom
- Institute for Islamic Studies
- Institute for Life and Family Studies
- Institute for Crisis, Dying, and Grief Counseling
- Institute for Pastoral Care

www.bucer.eu • info@bucer.eu

Berlin | Bielefeld | Bonn | Chemnitz | Hamburg | Munich | Pforzheim
Innsbruck | Istanbul | Izmir | Linz | Prague | São Paulo | Tirana | Zurich

www.ingramcontent.com/pod-product-compliance
Lightning Source LLC
Chambersburg PA
CBHW052104270326
41931CB00012B/2876